Top 40

Top 40

Brandon Brown

ROOF BOOKS
NEW YORK

ISBN: 978-1-931824-57-6
Library of Congress Control Number: 2014948655

Front cover design by Ben Sherry
Back cover photo by Kevin Killian

Thank you to J. Gordon Faylor, Kevin Killian, Susan Landers, Trisha Low, Cassandra Troyan, Dana Ward, and Alli Warren for their close and careful reading of this work.

 This book is made possible, in part, by the New York State Council on the Arts with the support of Governor Andrew Cuomo and the NYSCA New York State Legislature.

Roof Books
are distributed by
Small Press Distribution
1341 Seventh Street,
Berkeley, CA. 94710-1403
800-869-7553 or spdbooks.org

Roof Books
are published by
Segue Foundation
300 Bowery, New York, NY 10012
seguefoundation.com

Top Forty is for Dana, finally.

Top 40

All of a sudden, I break out laughing over the song that says "water will quench the thirst of the thirsty!" How did the singer arrive at this stunning discovery?

—Mahmoud Darwish
Memory for Forgetfulness

There are some motherfuckers I would like to show a star to

—Bernadette Mayer

KREWELLA, *LIVE FOR THE NIGHT*

For Kristopher "Rain Man" Trindl, Jahan Yousaf, and her sister Yasmine Yousaf, this is probably one of the best weeks of their lives, for their song *Live For The Night* is number #40 on America's Top 40 with Ryan Seacrest.

Because the Top 40 is listed in descending order, appearing first is technically the worst.

But it is the *Top* 40 after all.

If you find yourself after death living on the moon with the souls of the blessed who showed lack of fortitude in their earthly lives, who abandoned their earthly vows because of a small temerity of will, you're still technically in paradise, at least Dante's.

My brother has been trying to explain the convoluted scenario of the American League wild card right now on the Internet, and how the Kansas City Royals fit in it.

When people express confusion, he says, "They're the worst of the best."

I don't have a song on America's Top 40, but my week is going okay.

How's yours?

I go into the bathroom at work and spit into the urinal before I pee in it.

The spit has some blood in it and the blood gathers in the spare white water of the urinal, a suspended smudge.

Live For The Night is itself like a smudge of almost everything in pop music from the last few years.

It celebrates the allure and power of the night, a rarefied time marked by the disappearance of obligations to labor, which thus becomes the critical time to practice abandonment as a way of life, to supplant regular ascesis for a new, wilder one.

Living for the night in *Live For The Night* is figured as the loftiest practice possible, one worthy of so much devotion it becomes synonymous with existence.

In this way *Live For The Night* is ethical, in that if these three are going to live for the night, what are we going to do at night?

Saying "I live for X" is a classic dative of purpose.

I've been taking baths in the morning lately.

It started a few weeks ago when I was g-chatting with Ben.

Ben sent me a link to a piece that the fashion designer Tom Ford wrote for *Esquire,* in which he describes his toilette, the bejeweled minimalism of his opulent routines.

Ford takes several baths every day.

The first bath he takes is before his workout, right when he wakes up, he bathes with a glass of iced coffee, "slowly coming to life."

"I don't like hot beverages," he writes.

Reading the piece was so liberating, as I realized that I too don't really like hot beverages, and I vowed to introduce baths into my morning ablutions and drink iced coffee exclusively.

My bath is about ten minutes long or so, and I stare at the wall or ceiling, occasionally drawing my legs up and out of the water and stretching them along the facing plaster.

Or I lift my back from the bottom of the tub so that the water which rushes into the space my back had occupied is newly hot.

Yesterday morning I watched a cockroach glide along the trim, under a bad patch job over a kinky clump of mold.

I had never realized how graceful cockroaches can be.

I hardly ever see them, and up until yesterday morning I had only seen the stray bug at night, crumb-hunting in the kitchen.

Maybe this particular one was a "morning person."

I thought about getting out to smash its body into a smudge, but it felt weird, while "slowly coming to life" to be an agent of death, of any kind.

It's never pleasant to see cockroaches, unless you're at the house of some enemy, then you might relish it.

If I were Kristopher "Rain Man" Trindl, I might feel some anxiety about my job security.

For if anything drastic were to happen to the structural integrity of Krewella, I bet Kristopher is going to be the one to go, since after all Jahan and Yasmine are family.

"Krewella" is kind of clever, but I don't know about electing to use the infix nickname "Rain Man."

As a kid I was a frantic ranker and maker of lists, I kind of "lived for" making them.

I liked to make my own lists of pop songs, ranking all the ones I knew from worst to best.

One of my favorite things was Casey Kasem's America's Top 40, which I'd listen to every Sunday after church, buckled up in my parent's car, while they "socialized."

Church ended at 12:00, the time Kasem's show started, depending on the punctuality of the pastor and my success in avoiding sweet Lutherans, sometimes I'd miss the first, i.e. the 40th, song of the countdown.

Later I read an article about an autistic kid whose most obvious symptom was an obsession with America's Top 40.

He wrote down the top 40 songs in order every week and filed the loose papers in a homemade archive, for no one's use but his own.

It made me wonder.

TEGAN AND SARA, *CLOSER*

Today is Tegan and Sara's birthday!

It's also Filip's birthday.

Filip was in town for two weeks, I didn't see him, and I feel bad.

Filip, like Tegan and Sara, is a Virgo, and he wrote the most wonderful thing about Virgos recently, "Virgos are not organized chaos is."

Closer is set on the cusp between two bodies about to satiate their lust, its language is in the dialect of the sweaty threshold.

I guess Tegan and Sara typically have different objects of lust in their minds as they sing, even though they sing in unison.

For a long time I didn't know whether they were sisters, a couple, buddies, or what.

I have to admit that the reason I never paid much attention to them is because Logan liked them so much.

Logan is also a Virgo, like Filip, Tegan, and Sara.

Long ago, I made a hasty decision that our tastes were so radically different in their objects, that whenever Logan professed interest in a given work of art or artist I felt a sense of relief.

One less artist to have to attend to.

But now I dunno.

Closer makes a list of vows ("I won't treat you like you're typical") surrounded by a central imperative ("Come a little closer.")

Sometimes vows are more for the benefit of the vower than the avowed.

The vower experiences the narcissistic pleasure of making a promise he or she thinks is sooo charitable, as if not treating someone like they're typical is so hard.

The first word of the syntagm "I love you" is "I."

The word order matters, since "you are loved by me" is a different sentence.

Tegan and Sara were originally called Sara and Tegan, but flipped the names in interest of euphony.

It's not like we're supposed to think Tegan is superior to Sara or anything like that.

It's not that I thought I had superior taste to Logan, in fact, far from it, but rather that when it came to matters of taste we almost always differed.

I'm not even sure what taste is, so I don't know if it's something that can be "better" or "worse."

Taste is supposed to be something that there's no disputing, that is, something tautological, although in practice it is always the subject of dispute.

I don't think my taste is bad exactly, I just hate disputes so always admit it as for the gaudiest, most crystalline, obvious, normal art.

I'd rather read long lush descriptions of Tegan and Sara's haircuts than another page of Adorno ever.

But maybe this again is a matter of taste.

This afternoon I was talking to an acquaintance who said she was thinking about moving to a new neighborhood.

Being new to the Bay Area, she wondered about the various districts of San Francisco, and asked me for advice.

I said well what are you looking for in a neighborhood?

She said that she wanted to be around her age peers, be within walking distance to bars and boutiques, and to live in a place "where white people lived."

I made like a "I'm gonna throw up" face.

The meaning of the face was the opposite of the meaning of *Closer*, in that it meant "Please get farther away from me."

I was taken by surprise, and she, recognizing my discomfort, said ok byee and walked away.

I've spent the rest of the afternoon wondering what I should have said to her.

Some of my friends talk about "stringing people (capitalists) up," some talk about slitting throats in Oscar Grant Plaza, some joke about a server who was smashed in the face with a brick during a demonstration.

I guess such rhetoric makes Adorno look pretty chill, if no less annoying.

These sentences send me fleeing into Tegan and Sara's four arms, I come closer to them, I'm at their beck and call, they become my marshals, we support each other profoundly, bracingly, differently.

David often quotes Angela Davis, on the day of the General Strike in Oakland, saying "Our solidarities will be complex."

I don't want this tragic and horrible white person to be hanged for being so stupid, but I am okay with her going away from my door to never return.

My non-solidarity with her is simple; it's solidarity that's always more complex, like the molecules that make up a fungal ear on an old bathroom wall.

RIHANNA FT. MIKKY EKKO, *STAY*

I wrote a poem comparing Amanda Bynes to Socrates, Alli was like who is Amanda Bynes?

Her point I guess was that I rely too much on the endlessly substitutable icons of pop culture as catalysts for my writing, which could instead model itself after the timeless.

It's true that by the time I finish my book, much less by the time you're reading it, there will be an entirely new Top 40.

Cellular refiguration marked by rapid morphological mutation.

But there have always been poems made by reckoning the words and deeds of ephemeral heroes, like how poets shivered together in Viking Iceland, making metrical catalogs of blood some berserker spilled in the woods.

I like Rihanna's tenderness in *Stay*.

Like *Closer*, it is all about the desire for prolonged intimacy, but the discursive demand is softer.

It's not a command, but a hortatory expression of desire.

The difference between the imperative and the hortatory is figured in two of pop's most important tropes: "Let's Go" (hortatory) and "Come On" (imperative).

We went to a wedding over the weekend, it was beautiful, I cried.

I always do.

The night before the ceremony there was a barbecue, I got really high afterwards.

Sometimes when I get really high and the bed I'm sleeping in is nearby I say to my friends that I ought to go to bed and I do.

This was one of those nights.

But somebody downstairs had a guitar, and when they started playing

Kenny Rogers' *The Gambler*, the melody invaded my petrified REM and incited me back to the party.

The problem finally was that I was still high and couldn't remember the words to any of the verses to *The Gambler* or any of the other songs that we played, but the choral elements of all of them written into my RNA survived the memory-effacing effects of weed and a little sleep.

It was the best.

People really love singing together.

Rihanna's predicament in *Stay* is an inability to reconcile how to feel about her desire, a desire that trumps ambivalence but can't destroy it.

What she knows is she wants you to stay.

But she's "not sure how to feel about it," it being staying, considering the various kinds of despair and tedium the relationship includes.

On the other hand, her confusion is countervailed by a mysterious dance, "something in the way you move," a charismatic, almost undefinable kinesis which, perversely perhaps, settles in wanting you to stay.

If the simplicity of her desire in the end reminds you of Badiou's *Ethics*, you're remembering that the central exhortation of his book is much like what Rihanna says in *Stay:* continuez!

Simon Critchley, writing about Badiou and St. Paul, tries to summarize Badiou's thought, "Love binds itself to justice on the basis of hope.

The hope is that justice will be done and the subject maxim that this requirement of justice produces is, as elsewhere in Badiou, 'Continuez!'

That is, continue to love your neighbor as yourself.

That is, we might define hope as political love."

But "Stay" is also sung out of a melancholic trough allergic to permeation by light, what kind of love is it that we find there?

"When you never see the light it's hard to know which one of us is caving."

Context is critical to this ethical imperative (Badiou) or erotic hortatory (Rihanna.)

Because I do not want to say to the police "continuez."

I don't want to say anything to them which encourages their sustained presence in any way, unless they could be sustained as adorable little rodents with little bitty badges!!

Mostly I find crying contagious.

So when the groom or bride cries at a wedding, reading their vows, an elaborate way of formally reiterating "I want you to stay," water starts to redistribute in me.

I also lol'd.

It was at the worst possible moment, during the solemn and weepy trading rings.

A toddler a couple seats behind me asked her mother earnestly, hopefully, "Can I poop in my seat?"

When my friends' resolved faces collapsed in laughter, I had to laugh too.

I tried to tamp the outburst, first physically, holding my head in my hands, then by recalling how vastly inappropriate it was to laugh at *this* moment in the ceremony.

But maybe people just thought I was crying.

ROBIN THICKE ft. KENDRICK LAMAR, *GONNA GIVE IT 2 U*

It's easy to see why listening to *Gonna Give It 2 U* would cause instant and viral nihilism, but it is possible to resist.

That Thicke's song is hopeless doesn't mean that all efforts of art and life are doomed to travesty.

Gonna Give It 2 U's disaster is not that it shamelessly rehashes old and tired tropes, but that the tropes it rehashes are not old *enough*.

Poetry for me partakes of pre-literate measures of semiotic excess, the irreducible in human expression, that is, forgive me, hardly discernible from what we call the magical, and if it's something else for you, that's ok, but we are talking about different things when we talk about poetry.

When Parker died he left a note for his friends in a pair of black jeans.

His mom found them after he was gone and photocopied it for his closest friends.

He wrote, "I was somebody who believed in magic and love and basically got totally fucked."

Writing this book I am thinking a lot of Kathy Acker, who believed in magic, love, also got totally fucked.

She wrote, "In my confusion, I look to older writing, as I have often done when I am confused. I look to find a clue about my own writing."

Sometimes I think it would be great if we could trade a living Robin Thicke for a dead Kathy Acker.

Our world would be so much richer if only we could convince Robin Thicke to go down to Hel or Valhalla in the belief he has been sent to retrieve a lost hoard of Adderall and sunglasses, only to find, oops too late, he's been tricked.

And until recently, I was a Robin Thicke *advocate!*

To your objection that Thicke is a Schlitz to Justin Timberlake cognac, I'd simply have referred you to the many moments in which a Schlitz had made a miserable life more livable throughout its brief and flavorless duration.

But lately I dunno.

He seems to have strategized behavior which makes him impossible to claim, even as his success has never been brighter.

Part of what makes Thicke's efforts so impossible is that they seem to have taken on a new vocabulary encouraging sexual assault, which among other things spoils whatever sorts of seductive qualities they might have had.

I've recently figured out that I most respond to seduction in its two extreme forms: the most candid, and the most subtle.

In case you were planning on seducing me, now you know how I like it done.

In case U decide U want 2 give it 2 me.

My first experience of poetry in any form was pop music, which taught me about poetry and magic, love and fucking.

I have started reading the sagas because, confused, I intuit that reading the oldest forms of island thought will teach me something now about poetry and magic, love and fucking.

David gave me an edition of *Njal's Saga* right before Alli and I went to Iceland, but I never read it until now.

My favorite character so far is Olaf the Peacock.

His appearance is brief, but so cocky, so charitable, flamboyant, unforgettable.

You won't leave his house without a gift of a gold-inlaid spear or whatever.

OTP is buds with the wicked and taciturn Flosi, which I hope is pronounced "flossy."

"There was a man named Flosi, the son of Thord Frey's Godi, the son of Ozur, the son of Asbjorn, the son of Heyjang-Bjorn, the son of Helgi, the son of Bjorn Buna…Flosi's mother was Ingunn, the daughter of Thorir of Espihol, the son of Hamund Dark-skin, the son of Hjor, the son of Half who led Half's Warriors, the son of Hjorleif the Womanizer."

This is how a lot of *Njal's Saga* goes, lists of mostly male names, kinship relations, and epithets.

What kind of epithet should we give Robin Thicke as revenge for the shitty, sexist, unseductive art he's been making this year?

Robin Knucklebutt Fuckhead.

Robin Thicke is the son of Alan Thicke, who famously played a dad on TV.

Do you think it would be confusing to see your father play a father to a family of actors roughly your own age?

I wonder if he was a better dad to his TV family.

Njal's Saga is about a wise father, but as it was written hundreds of years after the events it purports to narrate, Njal's kids wouldn't have the chance to read heroic legends about the father who raised them in the merely semi-heroic real.

Not *so* many of my friends have become nihilists, despite the worldly appearance of *Gonna Give It 2 U.*

I haven't said anything about Kendrick Lamar's verse, which is deft and acrobatic but sounds a little too hasty to reflect a genuine crush.

I prefer glacial structures of feeling.

Drifting millimeter for a decade, you know it can't be wrong.

It's fine to flash, but if we really want 2 give it 2 each other there has to be more than shook foil between us.

Olaf the Peacock knew this too, even as he was putting "it" in your pocket.

FLORIDA GEORGIA LINE ft. NELLY, *CRUISE*

Never having driven a car, I have to project how much pleasure they must offer my sisters and fellows when they motor.

It must be a wonderful thing to do, a marvelous aesthetic practice.

For in *Cruise*, Brian Kelley, Tyler Hubbard, and Cornell "Nelly" Haynes, Jr. all share that the sight of a beautiful woman inspires in them one common desire: to roll down the windows of their respective cars, and drive them very fast.

Cruise conflates codes particular to both contemporary hip hop and contemporary country, regarding women and automobiles; in both, women are frequently described as little more than automobile accessories.

The car in these songs is a wickedly false object of allure to the imaginary female they intend to commodify.

It's like that house made of candy in *Hansel and Gretel,* you eat it because you're so hungry and it looks so delicious, but in the end, you just become food.

Cruise is indicative of a tendency in American pop music towards a homogeneity of codes, concerted attempts to dissolve genre, using different signifiers of course (Maybach vs. Chevy truck), and this homogeneity temporarily coheres in *Cruise* around the patriarchal apprehension of objects.

And thus, *Cruise* is a cracker-fried reiteration of traditional rap paeans to a wonderful car.

Okay, I lied, I have driven a car two times.

The first was in high school.

I was secretly dating my sister's best friend, one night they were sequestered in the bedroom talking and I snuck a note into the front seat of her car with instructions to park up the hill, and meet me by the door of my basement room.

My lust was poltergeistal, sifting through walls and settling like a horny dust all over the room.

When I heard them emerge, airily suggesting a drive into town, I panicked, raced her car down the street, stashed the note, returned to a trio of wtf.

I think this conditions my present disinclination to learn how to drive.

Because the fantasy of *Cruise* means little to me, every imagined scenario in which my driving arises is in the form of crisis.

"What if both my legs were broken and I needed a ride to the hospital," Alli asks, I shudder.

I dream about driving all the time.

They are always terrible durees of trenchant anxiety, my oneiric avatar screams until eyes open and sweat slicks my palms.

America's Top 40 suggests that the sudden sight of a beautiful body incites two kinds of responses: staying and fleeing.

People can be blasé about driving, they can be blasé about love, but not in America's Top 40, which is one reason it is better than us.

Blasé is contagious, addictive, and pop is the rehab clinic at which it is not okay to dabble.

Some people seemed surprised when they saw that Florida Georgia Line invited Nelly to make an appearance on *Cruise*.

But if the goal is to obliterate genre by imitation and incorporation, it makes sense to bring together the extremes.

I remember people always said, when asked what kind of music they listened to, "everything except rap and country."

My sisters really loved Nelly, and they listed to that *Country Grammar* song all the time.

Those Nelly songs didn't mean that much to me then, in fact I am more devoted to them now as delectable objects of ancient history, but I always liked that one of the guys in the St. Lunatics called himself "Chingy," a name too silly to evoke money.

Once at Erica's gallery I found a pencil drawing in the flat file of just Nelly's eyes.

Below the drawing of his eyes the artist had written the words "Nelly Eyes."

Now I can't remember who the artist is, and I've lost touch with Erica, so knowing my luck they're probably super famous.

The second time I drove a car was a few months ago in Alameda.

Alli really wants me to learn how to drive, it is one of the things I never seem to be able to give her and I know she is disappointed.

She took me to an old naval base with a huge parking lot so I could practice driving in her car.

I did okay I guess.

At one point I pulled up across from another car and we both stopped and looked at each other.

There was a dad in the passenger seat and a kid in the driver's seat, seriously, this kid looked like 12.

Like he was young enough to maybe never have heard of Nelly.

When he looked up at me, cramped and old in Alli's car, he shook his head with pity.

Maybe if I start to drive, I too will start to associate the sight of beautiful bodies with the desire for the open road, the window down, wind cruising across interior plush.

When I see beautiful bodies now, I just quiver and blush.

I rev or stall, in either case I fail to adequately respond to all that pretty information.

If I do ever have a car, I want one of those ones with curtains in the windows.

THE NEIGHBOURHOOD,
SWEATER WEATHER

I bet these dudes in the Neighbourhood think their dreamy mid-tempo *SweaterWeather* is the antithesis of the grim, souped-up fantasy of *Cruise,* a Jeff Koons to its Jeff Gordon.

But it does not dream of a world better than the one those guys cruise in.

It might even be more grim.

Cruise doesn't pretend to have any elusive agenda; they objectify women, drive cars, exult in their identities, call it a day.

Sweater Weather too begins by establishing all the familiar integers of a masculine worldview.

"All I am is a man / I want the world in my hands."

As the boys in the Neighbourhood, or NBHD as they like to stylize it, turn their gaze on the specific object of their lust, they bewail the beauty of the natural world, maybe because they passionately hate whatever eludes their grasp.

Jesse Rutherford sings, "I hate the beach."

Just say those words "I hate the beach," feel how they adapt to the shape of your mouth and your laryngeal functions.

Hatred of the beach is a powerful symbol of an abject relationship to what's good in the world, preferring plaint over pleasure.

Maybe if you masochistically live in Boston or Chicago or some-place like that you can sublimate your own climactic resentment until it extends to all ecosystems however beautiful, but I don't recommend it.

Better to moisturize the eczema of the nerve endings around the heart.

It's autumn, but the beginning of autumn in Oakland ironically brings about a caesura in sweater weather.

Sometimes I feel nervous when I see people wearing sweaters or bulky jackets when it's too hot to be wearing anything like that.

Like our sensibilities could not possibly partake of a common world.

At the wedding Michael said he hates being in a hot tub.

I was speechless (for once).

I mean, he said he has eczema, which is exacerbated by water so hot.

Still, what?

Stephanie and Clive went to Vichy Hot Springs before the wedding, a famous hot springs that announces itself as "Jack London's Favorite Hot Springs."

I had never heard of it, but since the wedding I've seen the billboards in Oakland for the hot springs so many times, it's as if Stephanie and Clive summoned the place into optics.

They have what are called "champagne" bubble baths, the champagne in quotes because the water is merely carbonated, not alcoholic, although you can apparently drink it.

So you simultaneously wash and slurp.

Today on the bus, four young guys sat in a cloud of weed.

One of them played pop music from a phone.

They sang and laughed, danced in their seats, high and happy.

I liked them, they were so vulnerable in their love for the tunes and each other's company.

When Miguel's *Adorn* came on I heard another voice join them.

I turned and made eye contact with a young woman, singing along, I thought is this whole bus going to start singing together.

I'm glad my curiosity didn't deter her, misread as a weird gawk.

People really love to sing together.

Going to the beach can also be a kind of asceticism.

Curing the body with salt, opens pores, makes the body permeable to new and unthought pleasures.

"I hate the beach," Jesus.

Even Mord Fiddle, Sighvat the Red's prick son, even *his* ugly lips curled up, laying out on a long towel west of the westernmost fjords.

"I hate the sky, I hate the smell of cannabutter, I hate the taste of clean water, I hate Katy Perry, I hate sound, I hate the tingle that wraps from the spine over the skull when orgasm approaches but has not yet crested."

This guy used to come in the café every night, he wore a leather jacket, and the same white Sonic Youth shirt, and he always ordered tea, which he brought to his mouth haltingly, shaking, although he looked too young for a tremor.

He was mean and surly, and we, the staff, didn't like him, and we mocked him behind his back and mocked the way his hands shook when he tried to lift the tea, because we were vicious and young and our hands had not yet shook.

Once he asked one of the baristas what they did outside of work, and when she said she was an artist, he wrinkled his nose and made a face.

There was a pause and then he said, "I hate art."

DRAKE, *HOLD ON WE'RE GOING HOME*

If I were listening to America's Top 40 with Ryan Seacrest live, the appearance of *Hold On, We're Going Home* would be a prompt to turn the volume up, way up.

Especially following the unearned and misguided pathos of *Sweater Weather.*

That's part of what lends a countdown its particular suspense; you can't tell the future.

But I'm not listening to the Top 40 in one extended sitting, instead I stray, revisit, lurch forward and backward across its span, walking to the train, waiting for the bus, little crystal rhomboid serenading me.

Hold On We're Going Home is so pretty it's hard to attend to what it's even saying (not much.)

It's kind of perverse, but I mostly listen to it precisely at the time that I *leave* my own home to *go* to work.

Playing it then repudiates the real, makes a harmonic contrafactual.

It's autumn, you can tell, the light has really changed in the morning.

Each morning looks ever darker, stubbornly rotting plum, I shower, it weakens.

Fernand Braudel wrote, "Financialization is a sign of Autumn."

Baseball season is almost over, financialization is almost over, Drake and I are almost over.

Drake is the contemporary theorist of the "one life" model of living, when life is over will Drake be.

He sings, "It's hard to do these things alone" and he could mean almost anything by "things."

Go home, go out, participate in the disastrous delirium of finance, flee from it in a shabby boat; it's easier if we collectivize and don't try to do these things alone.

I've gotten to the part of *Njal's Saga* which is a long court transcript, an ornate analysis of debt resolution.

It turns out the family can be really unhomely.

Just ask Njal, who spent all his free time settling blood debts accrued by his kids.

One of the things I love in Kathy Acker's writing is how ruthlessly she is able to divorce herself from her family and describe the new one, fucked up and unpredictable as it is, that arrives in its place.

This morning I saw the headline of the paper said that Oakland is now the robbery capital of the United States.

A friend got mugged last week in the neighborhood, so scary.

I went out on the fire escape to smoke.

There was a woman across the way, also smoking, on her stoop.

A guy weaved down the street, he looked like me in the sense that he was white and full of wine.

She and I looked at him, then looked at each other, back at him, back at each other, as if to say I really hope this weaver gets home safely.

It's hard to do these things alone.

I wish he had had a weaving-down-the-street buddy.

Sometimes deciding the end of the night has arrived is lamentable, but sometimes not.

Sometimes you decide to go home and find it permits something unexpected and wonderful, the bed or floor suddenly alluring, like the nasty backseat of a taxicab suddenly accommodates overweening lust you barely knew had even weened.

But it's almost always better to have somebody say hold on we're going home and take you home.

Nietzsche writes, "From the sun I learned this: when he goes down, over-rich; he pours gold into the sea out of inexhaustible riches so that even the poorest fisherman still rows with golden oars."

Hold On We're Going Home is about the desire for reciprocal love that never sloughs off the intensity and heat of its inception.

It proposes simultaneous and paradoxical stability ("hold on") and motion ("we're going home") as the outcome of a desire which, by achieving its object ("your hot love and emotion"), negates the possibility of this achievement effecting satisfaction ("endlessly").

I got so paranoid Saturday night going home from Woolsey, having indulged in a last long draw off smoldering spliff, riding back to Alli's place I freaked.

First, I thought we'd be robbed on the way to the car.

Next, that we'd careen drunk, collide with another car crossing double lines, our bodies sheared like blades through necks in ancient Iceland.

Finally that Alli's car would lose control, flip onto its top, glue our heads along the hardness of the street.

In Drake's work he often describes "starting from the bottom" before a quasar-like explosive leap to the cashy echelons, his current domicile.

Almost nothing feels better in the moment as pure gullibility and almost nothing feels stupider in hindsight.

Everybody knows that Drake did not start from the bottom.

It's weird to think of a teenager holding golden oars but I just did it.

AWOLNATION *SAIL*

Aaron Bruno got the nickname "AWOL" in high school because of his habit of disappearing silently and suddenly from parties.

Although I make it a habit to dissociate from the martially-inclined, I actually did know somebody who went AWOL from the Marines, having made a rash decision to join after high school and immediately regretting it.

Before reporting to basic training, he tried to injure himself into a discharge.

He strapped a potato to his knee for the whole summer, he told us this was supposed to somehow produce a simulacrum of water-on-the-knee.

When that didn't work, Santino ran over his foot with a car, shattering his phalanges and metatarsals.

When he still failed to win a discharge, he finally went AWOL from basic training in Santa Barbara, lived on the beach for a while before he was apprehended, briefly jailed, dishonorably released.

Sail has been in and out of the Top 40 for a full two years now, sailing into its voluptuous harbor and flushing back out again, going AWOL, and then reappearing like a ghost ship out of the fog.

I had never heard it before now, writing this book.

But it is immediately familiar.

Sail pays homage to classic grunge self-debasement, richly abject and extensively self-loathing.

And yet its abjection is marked by a significant difference from the canonical 90's moan.

Where Kurt Cobain's psychic pain was that of a depressive opiate addict, Aaron Bruno blames his suicidal inclination on ADD.

I dunno, I think I suffer most from what I can't avoid attending.

Shower twinge.

Airport dew.

I'm always thinking about the cow in Nietzsche's book about history, big grimy teeth, covered in cud, decidedly *not* worried about his or her behavior at the afterparty.

I took Adderall for the first time this summer at Woolsey.

I had been sipping white wine all day, aggregated splashes and nips, celebrating Anne's birthday, baking in a sun transfigured by the supersolar radiance of Anne and the promise of her continued existence.

But by ten, after Chris and Aaron read but before Wendy, I was fading.

I told a friend, "I'm kind of fading."

They asked me if I had any heart problems.

I said I didn't think so?

You already probably know this, seasoned reader, but Adderall is pretty wonderful, breezy focus sails in with minimal turbulence, it worked so fast and gently in me I began to suspect it was a placebo effect, no drug could be this good.

After the reading I walked onto the porch to smoke with Andrew and Shon and I said, "Man, this Adderall is great."

Shon said, "Uh oh."

I didn't really feel like I was even that high but when Alli and I were in bed she said I couldn't stop talking.

Sail is extremely minimal in its message.

There are a couple declarative sentences, a couple rhetorical questions, and an imperative ("Sail into the dark with me.")

I guess I date myself as pure 90's, ever associating a sail into darkness with an opiate blanket.

I don't think I have whatever ADD is which is apparently why Adderall feels superbly clarifying and transformative.

It doesn't really feel that "dark" to me.

Maybe Aaron Bruce is hearkening to a shadowy 19th century drug narrative, eliding the affective differences in the various pharm.

It's easy to understand the 19th century of drugs as a dark river, since that's how all those 19th century druggies understood it too.

I'm pretty good at doing drugs, but I am really bad at asking people for them, which is why so many years went by before I even tried Adderall.

But don't worry, I'm not going to get addicted to it.

This summer, Michael told me about an ex-girlfriend who smoked so much pot, which is hardly a drug I know strictly speaking, but that she smoked so much pot, like wake and bake every day, and my first question, which I asked in an innocent, curious, not judgmental way, was did you guys ever have sex when she wasn't high and he said no.

Keston Sutherland writes, "Our tribute to the world is our desire, nothing else."

I guess that includes the desire for self-obliteration, the desire to navigate one's life into the refuge of darkness, the desire to post up forever in a cavern, swatting a drugyata until it splits.

Tributes have always been moneyed, even the most generous, there is always a forethought of debt.

If there is a tribute in *Sail* it is a Seattle of tributes, slick and gloomy.

PINK ft. NATE RUESS, *JUST GIVE ME A REASON*

Because of you, my loneliness is only burlesque.

I can't believe that one of us will almost surely die before the other.

I will love dead you too although I hope to never meet her.

Love formally accommodates feeling in excess of prescriptive, governable, euphonious measures.

As our measures can be ungovernable and dysphonic, so can our love be.

Ungovernability can also be ascetic, a way of life.

This is the one poem in this book that's for you, not you all.

Like a song comes on the radio, a disc jockey's peaty voice intones, "This one goes out to Alli from BB, pining across the lake."

Then Lionel Richie (or whoever) singles you out from the unknowable crowd of listeners, crooning code, hello.

Form is what tries to lord over love, it always admits it, completely fails.

A lot of my friends really love this essay called "Against the Couple Form" by Clementine X. Clementine.

"Against the Couple Form," argues that there is no couple that can exist without an original sexual violence, as long as patriarchal conditions obtain, and that polyamory is not a sufficient challenge to structures of possession historically embedded in gender relations.

And I get it, and I am more or less against the couple form too.

Except I am hardly ever really against anyone's happiness if their happiness includes some revolt against the horrors of the origin and form, if it tries at least to deny that sentence.

Also I fucking *love* duets, don't you?

I am desperate to forget how pervasive this originary violence of the couple form is whenever I think about being in love with you.

We even sing well together, in a sense, although you've always misinterpreted my comparing your singing voice to Daniel Johnston's a veiled insult, it's not.

Our harmony, like all harmony, is the effect of real alterity, I'm another tongue in you, we will always be apart, connected by the tongue when we are, hello, it's how we continue each other.

There can be others, there are and will be others, a choir surrounds us, flirty wet and hard and choirsome, no matter how squishy you or I get inside it I will always parse your voice in its chorus.

Just Give Me A Reason is the tale of two lovers in a rut, who want desperately to stay together.

Each asks the other to give them a reason to stay, a pretense as love like poetry has nothing or almost nothing to do with reasons.

I sit in the library on my lunch break sipping iced tea, trying to think of similes to describe Nate Ruess's voice.

I don't get very far.

"Bloodless chestnut?"

"Bay of (no) rage?"

Sometimes when we dip into a rut and I'm being a broody bitch I think will I be mad about this when I'm dead, wrestling a wolf in Hel.

I should be more generous to Nate Ruess.

It's not his fault Pink is a Jupiter and he merely a moon.

Love is reciprocal orbitality, planets and moons taking turns being magnets.

Will you marry me or is that stupid?

When they sing "Just a little bit's enough" it's so true, so well-known, but it's so desperate here I'm moved.

In Hel all you do is yearn to come back to earth a molecule of spit.

If I die first I will continue in you, even if I wane into almost no cells, dead skin, shit, that will be how I love you from Hel, Valhalla, wherever I end up, there will be a smell in the air, kush oxygen of Oakland, something earthy from a fault in the dirt.

Why can't I write a valentine that doesn't have shit in it?

I am slime, I will always be your baby.

In the bathroom at work, someone threw a wadded piece of toilet paper on the floor.

The shit on it was thick and brown, it really popped off the austere white.

It was like the impasto of Courbet's painting.

No one touched it, of course, but near the end of the day, some-one, revolted into poiesis, made a sign, and taped it on the wall.

They drew a downward arrow and wrote, "WHAT THE FUCK IS THIS???"

I'm trying to say I love you is the repeated rhetorical excess of the shock that this can be possibly so, reasonlessly true.

PINK ft. LILY ALLEN *TRUE LOVE*

If I could meet one figure from world mythology, I think it would have to be Idunn, Braggi's wife, who tends a basket of apples that the Gods eat when they notice signs of aging, the apples make them young again.

I could use another half a life to work on my book about truth, love, violence, poetry, Old Norse poetics, and America's Top 40.

Last night Alice Notley read a line like "Age isn't about time, it just *happens.*"

I go into the bathroom at work and spit into the urinal before pissing.

There's no blood but a dark streak wedged between tiny bubbles.

True Love is a quintessential Pink song, for Pink typically carries only two messages for the men in her purview, there are manifold examples of each.

One, you want me, but you're a prick, and go fuck yourself.

Two, you want me, you're a prick, but I can't help myself I'm yours.

The key to the latter message is that love brings about surrender; love and hate both involve drastic duress that makes breathing difficult.

In this way Pink's work scales the long range from ambivalence to ecstasy, from narcissism to alterity, which is also the title of my memoir.

I'm actually "in hate" with someone right now.

Realizing that I was in hate didn't make me feel great, its intensity made me realize that I hadn't been in hate for a long time, not really.

I can tell I hate this person because I had a fantasy just now about reading this poem in their presence, after which they would approach me and ask if they were the person I hated in my poem about *True Love* and I would say oh god, of *course not*, X, it's not you, but it would be them, and I am pleased by having both vented and concealed my hate.

I guess I must have loved them once.

Hate too appears as a twinge in the upper chest, same as love.

But I would not call my hate for this person true love.

Aristotle says that the true friendship is the one that does not partake of economies, that it consists of a love for which reciprocity is not simply missing but irrelevant.

Avital Ronell writes of the other in this scheme as a "rigorous no-show."

These relationships are ordinary, you hear this all the time, "I give and I give and I get nothing back."

But these friendships, in which one person gives and gives and the other feels no charge to return affection or care, I would call these bad, or like fucked up, friendships.

Pink's proposal in *True Love*, "I hate you, I really hate you, so much it must be…true love," is an ancient poem, easy to know but a little hard to believe.

What makes us want to believe it?

Do you think Gangleri believed everything he heard about Hnoss, who was so beautiful that everything which is beautiful and precious in the world is called *hnossir* (treasures) after her?

Pink is so clinically theatrical.

This song sounds like a convertible top pulling back on a bright afternoon, its movements are mechanical and slow, but it makes the whole world a waterfall.

Lily Allen's cameo is superfluous but fine.

A little "girl, I hear you…" which every real plaint about painful simultaneity desires, since there is after all no possible resolution.

I feel strange admitting that I hate someone, like you'll think I'm a monster.

Pretend that this is a fiction and that I love this person and everybody, ok?

Pink pulls negativity off so flawlessly, fierce but playful, whereas in my poem it just feels nasty.

Or maybe you all know the feeling too and sympathize?

OK, either remember how you hate someone and sympathize or pretend it's a fiction, deal?

Pink's album is called *The Truth About Love*.

Love and hate are unlike taste in that love and hate are true, where taste is tautological and thus has no relationship with truth.

To the objection that her work is not a valid contribution to the philosophical tradition which has taken up love as an object of inquiry, I'd simply say something obvious, which is that pop is for many of us a prerequisite course in the regime of signs by which we understand what these signifiers, like love and hate, even mean.

I got home late last night, walking from the train, I didn't see anyone out, I started to feel a little scared.

You can't predict the future, only try to clock its inflections in the present as best you can.

But it's not easy to tell the present either, what the meaning of the smoke smell in the air is, whether the surging wind is insignificant or if it foreshadows stirring below the earth's crust, fell trunks, what it all means to live in the "the robbery capital of the United States," what is an earworm, what is one brick in a Foot Locker's shitty window.

When I got home, I exhaled hard, in hindsight my anxiety was idiotic.

If anyone reading this is "in hate" with me, you can reflect on this moment with pleasure, you jerk.

LABRINTH ft. EMELI SANDE, *BENEATH YOUR BEAUTIFUL*

No need to tell Timothy McKenzie, who performs under the nom de plume "Labrinth," that not only has he misspelled "Labyrinth" in his name, but that you think the "your" in *Beneath Your Beautiful* ought to be "you're," he's heard it.

He's protested that the song's eccentric orthography is purposive, to drive English teachers and quote grammar Nazis unquote insane.

If you insist on considering his title a mere error, one might also say the song could be called *Beneath Your Beauty,* as if beauty were ever an overlay for something more than itself.

Instead, the syntax suggests that McKenzie's desire is not solely for the possessor of beauty, but for whatever could possess what is meaningless without an object, the roaming adjective.

I used to walk the labyrinth at Grace Cathedral all the time.

Before I went there, I had visualized a three dimensional structure, rising hedges higher than my head, an immersive, swallowing structure.

But I was confusing a labyrinth with a *maze*.

A labyrinth is devotional, reverent, a demarcated space for prayer with only one possible geometry.

On the other hand, a maze is a puzzle intentionally difficult to navigate and supposed to entrap its passengers.

Part of the confusion is of course that the original labyrinth, in Crete, was actually a maze that the Cretans called "labyrinth."

From where Grace Cathedral and its labyrinth lie on the top of Nob Hill, San Francisco splays out, expansive and expensive below.

If you are very concentrated while walking you can ignore the towering palaces of those thieves who transformed Nob Hill into a high Versailles.

Beneath Your Beautiful uses spatial and directional imagery to suggest naughtiness, like when he says he wants to see beneath your beautiful and take a look "inside."

The lack of a noun makes "beautiful" anchorless and thus potentially applies to whatever the listener wants to imagine occupies the syntactic absence.

"Please let me see beneath your beautiful (clothes)"

"Please let me see beneath your beautiful (palace)"

"Please let me see beneath your beautiful (notebook)"

There's a tall building in *Beneath Your Beautiful* too, tall as the Fairmont.

"I'm gonna climb on top your ivory tower / I'll hold your hand and then we'll jump right out."

This weekend was the conference on poetry and revolution at various Universities of California.

I woke up late Saturday morning, not hungover but definitely droopy.

When the bus dropped me off at the campus gates, the marching band had gathered with hundreds of football fans to march to the field.

I fumbled my way through their mass, a calculated look of disdainful and elitist horror on my face, so hypocritical, as I love sports.

I had loudly proclaimed to many of my friends that I was not going to attend the poetry and revolution conference, that nothing could drag me to campus on my day off, that I felt alienated from the milieu convening the conference, that I'd be better off sitting in my apartment reading a book or drinking iced tea, or taking a long bath, or doing almost anything, but when I woke up I realized my invective had been careless and stupid, went, and had an extraordinary time.

I know, I suck, I learned a ton.

Francesca's talk was about "revolutionary tenderness," a form of care that doesn't naively eradicate antagonism, instead proposes that discursive challenges could be elaborated tenderly, that real radical permission can have its source in finding more open modes of being together.

I thought of Otis Redding of course and his expansive intelligence, try a little tenderness.

How his tenderness ended up snuffed in that lake in Madison we all went nightswimming in, when Anna told us it was the lake Redding's plane crashed in we all went ugh.

Alli and I had some time alone between the panels and the reading.

I put on *Beneath Your Beautiful*, guessing that Alli would appreciate, if nothing else, McKenzie's vocal performance, his rasp in the chorus reminiscent of Joe Cocker, one of her favorite singers.

She paused on the top of the stairs, considering.

"Beneath your beautiful?"

We both laughed at how stupid the phrase was and life.

We referenced other silly lines from poems and songs, lines so gross we've repeated them for years, how they are miserably unforgettable, overfull of meaning.

They are some of our favorite things to say to each other.

I'm not sure it's so tender of us to tease these lines and their authors in our little lover's language.

But they are so hostile to mystery they bind us in mutual indignation.

There is no mystery in the message of *Beneath Your Beautiful* either, and in that way it too is like a labyrinth, not a maze.

Labrinth himself is only *like* a labyrinth, what without that "y."

But when his voice scrapes on that note in the chorus, I feel decidedly less lost.

LORDE, *ROYALS*

America's Top 40 attempts to draw a matrix of collective attention in the present.

Its definition of "the present" is the week.

I've been reading *The Seven Day Circle: The History and Meaning of the Week* by Eviatar Zerubavel, it's pretty good.

Zerubavel suggests that wherever there is a "week," which is most places, with various lengths, this week provides a temporal "beat" by which members of a given culture experience time.

Max Weber adds that the week emerges in the west concomitant with market days, the recurring opportunity to shop musically organizes what is known as the week.

So the weekly structure of America's Top 40 rides that beat, inextricable from the marketplace and its logic, its structure fitted precisely to a culture obsessed with competition and rank.

There's something desperate about it too in how it strives week after week to canonize the contemporary.

Its challenge will always be that the Top 40, as with the law of fashion which states that the moment one is in fashion one is therefore out of fashion, begins to fossilize the moment it finally coheres.

But some things appear to never change.

Like the fact that there are royals.

Royals is the first song so far in the Top 40 to be *about* the Top 40.

Pop has been suggested in other places, it decorates the rhetorical longing in *Cruise,* for instance, but neither the guys in Florida-Georgia Line nor Nelly criticize its content as such.

In *Royals,* the content of the Top 40 is brought into relief as a negative form of life against which Ella Yelich-O'Conner and her friends oppose themselves.

I'm not sure how much I am persuaded by the insistence that they aren't "caught up in the love affair," the satire is so pretty as it recapitulates the themes of contemporary royalty.

That is of course the morbidly catchy genius of what it critiques.

I like when her voice doubles, trebles, how the richness of its sound reiterates the richness it antagonizes.

Lorde wants to convince us that her reign will be magnanimous and sweet.

But I dunno.

Some of my friends who want to "string people (capitalists) up," or slit throats in Oscar Grant Plaza, or joke about the server smashed in the face with a brick during a demonstration, those friends are mostly magnanimous and sweet too.

Lorde's methods are questionable, no doubt, but I think she agrees with us that we don't want our poems to meekly praise aristocrats.

People really love to sing together.

In *Prose Edda*, Snorri Sturluson describes the origin of poetry.

Aegir, Norse god of ocean parties, asks Bragi, god of poetry, where did poetry come from?

Bragi replies, "The origin of it is that the gods had a dispute with the people called Vanir, and they appointed a peace-conference and made a truce by this procedure, that both sides went up to a vat and spat their spittle into it.

But when they dispersed, the gods kept this symbol of the truce and decided not to let it be wasted, so made a human being out of the spit, named it Kvasir.

Kvasir was so wise that no one could ask him any question to which he did not know the answer.

He traveled the world, famous for being smart.

Then two dwarves invited him over to their house and killed him.

They poured his blood into two pots, mixed honey with his blood, and the honey-blood mixture became a mead that makes whoever drinks it into a poet.

This is why we call poetry "Kvasir's blood" or "dwarfs' drink" or "the contents" or some term for "liquid of Odrerir" or "Bodn" or "son," or "dwarf's transportation."

The enthusiasm I had for ranking as a kid thankfully waned but I did continue to count.

I count minutes down near the wane of every work day.

I count strokes, breaths, and laps when I swim.

I count sentences in my book *Top Forty*.

One of the best things about *Royals* is that it makes negativity a celebration by taking such pleasure in the word "never."

And yet I have often had the weak daydream that the very success of *Royals* has made Ella Yelich-O'Conner unimaginably rich, I hope and think that she will be okay and never be a royal.

Do you think *Royals* could be used as a fight song for the Kansas City Royals?

I mean, after all, no other song that I can think of has ever emphasized so lushly the world *Rooooyals*.

Americans like to pretend we don't have them.

I guess unfortunately for the Royals *Royals* says "We'll *never* be royals."

ICONA POP ft. CHARLI XCX, *I LOVE IT*

Taste probably starts tickling fetal buds through pores in the placental sack, but we usually start articulating it during puberty, zits pop out of the skin like they had always been there, incubating, waiting for their moment of recognizability, just in time to ruin love.

Always mutable, taste burlesques as a permanent filter for the senses and the objects of sense.

An audit of what tastes good at any moment, that is, feels definitive, permanent, a rash you think will never go away, waxing hour after a long hit of kush that appears to extend infinitely into the future, you feel you will never not be high.

On the train this morning, I kept touching the skin of my cheeks and chin to see if I could "feel redness," ugh.

I didn't have a mirror, but became convinced my face had become roseate, covered over with barely perceptible welts.

I'm addicted to thinking about these welts, as meaningless and unhelpful as thinking about them is, obsessing about them is the only available balm.

This summer, I listened to *I Love It* compulsively, at least once a day, usually several times.

Often I would play it twice in a row, three times, renewably buoyed by the filthy noise of its opening note, how it warns its hearer of how much dirty pleasure awaits.

I Love It considers a set of irreconcilable differences between the pitiful addressee and the fierce trio of Caroline Hjelt, Aino Jawo, and Charli XCX.

They condescend from the Milky Way whereas you live on earth.

Memorably, you are from the 70's but they are a 90's bitch.

To love something but not care is like Aristotle's concept of true friendship, tenderless solidarity between citizens.

I Love It hypothesizes that not caring can make love more not less robust, that not caring can be the object of our most passionate feelings.

At the poetry and revolution conference, Jennifer said that the poetry community is a place where you often do a lot of work with people you don't necessarily like, you can love and not care, or sometimes you do care, too much.

You know how in *The Prelude,* Wordsworth rows a boat out onto a moonlit pond, awed by the susurrations of cattails in the lunar lit breeze and the poem latently suggests this experience was formative to his later development as a poet?

Well, for me it was just like that, only I wore headphones and there was nothing "natural" anywhere in sight.

When I started writing poetry as a teen in the early 90's, I wrote about feelings of abjection and ecstasy.

My writing worried about love and friendship, sex and death.

I listened to pop music whose message was very frequently "I love it" and "I don't care."

The books I loved most were always either dirty and wretched or supple and lush beyond good taste or all these things at once.

In other words, not much has changed.

This might be TMI but I have entertained the thought that this rash, which has spread red across the tender skin of my neck and now face (fuck!!!!), has its source in caring too much.

The dirt on my shoulder would fill a graveyard, no shovel big enough to slough it all off.

Some say friendship is based on the attraction of like to like, that the friend is "the familiar other," the one who agrees with you on the social, political, and artistic questions of the day.

What do you think?

In Plato's *Lysis,* Socrates and his horny friends go to the gym to cruise lithe naked youths.

He engages a couple of them in a conversation about friendship, and this little *ménage a trois* considers whether friendship is based on the attraction of like to like, the unlike to the unlike, whether the friend is good, bad, or neutral.

Socrates proposes a final but not conclusive model, that the friend is *oikeios,* or "of the house," home-ly.

The friend who is of-the-house is not a sympathetic other but somebody who is simply native to us, the friend is the person we feel we've known forever the moment we meet.

This Socratic metaphor is, you know, "homie."

I guess the problem for Caroline and Aino and all of us is to determine what constitutes our "house."

Unlike the house which is by definition stable, taste always upsets its foundation, has no discernible origin, it emerges only to disappear whenever it wants, luggage up in a dumpster, then back on a plane.

It's like the Milky Way, you can see it from a distance, but what can you say conclusively about it?

Masha Tupitsyn writes, "Taste is tribalistic.

Taste is inheritance.

A hand-me-down."

I Love It wears its genetic heritage obstinately.

I love it and I care about it, and I am indebted to Charli XCX, the woman who wrote it.

But what's up with that name, Charli XCX?

Are they supposed to be Roman numerals?

BONNIE MCKEE, *AMERICAN GIRL*

It turns out "XCX" being Roman numerals is the last thing anybody thinks "XCX" stands for in Charli XCX's name.

What would be subjunctively good about that, though, is that "XC" is how you'd write 90 (C, 100, minus X, 10) but the extra "X" after "XCX" would then add the 10 back to 90 so you'd have 100 again.

That's the algebra for home-ly love, that in discovering the other who appears to complete your life, you find that they had always been *missing*, that you'd been living a life in want, walking minus ten at least.

Charli herself insists that the XCX is pure ornament, an improvised and meaningless placeholder for nothing at all, she only jokes it stands for "kiss cunt kiss."

I'm stalling, disappointed with *American Girl*.

Bonnie McKee has written so many indelible pop songs that I simply expect everything she does to be a fireworks finale.

Nothing in this world matters less whether I like *American Girl* or not; my "disappointment" is just as pathetic as the pride I might potentially feel, she has helped make some of the world's finest art.

American Girl indexes a number of quintessential traits supposed to describe Americans of any sex.

"I was raised by a television / Every day's a competition."

In theory I would support Bonnie McKee becoming a sovereign dictator over the whole world, but the platform she adumbrates in *American Girl*, sensory deprival and extravagant competition, seems too much like the old world of dicks.

Some say that *American Girl* describes an America that's neutralized its sensibility by replacing the parent with the device, an America so alienated from forms of cooperation that a day without competition is impossible to imagine, and thus the song constitutes a critique of those facts.

But I dunno.

Why do I feel the need to make Bonnie McKee my avenger against capital and state violence, what did she ever do, what's wrong with me?

To make myself laugh, I imagined *American Girl* transposed in the Iceland of the sagas.

"I'm an old Icelandic girl / woah-oh."

"I was raised by Guðrun-deep-minded / every day is full of crazy Vikings / woah-oh-oh"

OK now you go.

Today on the bus everybody started coughing at once.

Packed in, I was sitting beneath the sudden and multiple sounds of harsh exhales, bursting glottises, expectorate sailing out into hands, I hope, mottled air, bacterial seat, back of my hair.

It was gross, I put my headphones on.

It was, perhaps, the most USAmerican thing I did all day, My Immunist Manifesto, trying to make *American Girl* an echinaceal apotrope.

Kathy Acker writes, "The world is sick.

Why?

No reason.

Since there's a monster in it."

American Girl ecstatically reifies US foreign policy, infantile but no less terrifying thereby, like a baby with a hot iron walking around, super cute but like *super* fucked up.

She's okay with being the monstrous child, "I never listen to mommy / I never say that I'm sorry."

Tom Petty also has a song called *American Girl*, a quite good one.

For a while I was a young heartbroken guy living with three other young heartbroken guys in a dilapidated one bedroom apartment in the Haight; it was a real shit-show.

The floors were thin and our downstairs neighbor, Judah, hated our guts.

Remind me to tell you about the time we went to the music store where he worked, he had to tune our fiddle and mandolin.

One night John came in Matthew's room at two a.m. and said, "I just ran into Judah and he asked us to play *American Girl* as loud as we could."

We were too drunk and heartbroken to disbelieve him.

Later, we threw out a week's cigarette butts out the window.

Judah had draped his clothes on the fire escape to dry, ash settled on them like mountain snow.

In the lyric complaint he left on our doorstep he wrote THE WORLD IS NOT YOUR ASHTRAY.

Bonnie McKee's *American Girl* is about how foreign such a thought was to us, as American guys, the world totally felt like our ashtray.

We didn't apologize then, but now I feel a little bad.

When we brought in the fiddle and the mandolin to get tuned, he twisted the strings into tune with impressively stoic dispassion, hate burbling just beneath his grit teeth.

Sadistic and "American guy" as it is to admit, the look on his face when we walked in to the music store with a fiddle and mandolin, as he foresaw a future of very unneighborly behavior, that shit still makes me laugh to the present day.

SELENA GOMEZ, *COME AND GET IT*

"Come and get it" was the familiar exhortation my family used to announce that a meal had been prepared and was ready to eat.

It was a formal call to reproduce ourselves sociocalorically.

The dinners were eaten rapidly and silently.

I did have this "put my head in my hands and cry during dinner" phase but it was pop-song brief relative to a couple decades of going and getting it.

It's a cliché that Midwesterners are supposed to be nice and everyone in my family was nice.

They were nice to people whether they liked them or not.

Maybe it's all that church, in the way that church is a social form where people collaborate with each other all the time, and yet it doesn't really matter whether they like each other or not, their solidarity around a theory of God's charity trumps taste.

Although manners are so flimsy, collapse under stress, in the church or with poets.

I always considered myself an extremely nice person but this summer Sophie said I was kind of a dick actually, but I dunno.

Maybe I was acting like a dick all summer?

Come And Get It starts with a tabla beat and a voice singing in Hindi, before Selena Gomez's voice charges through robotic braces, imploring the object of her desire to come and get it.

Her singing exudes swagger and confidence, ironic since the content of the song suggests handing over autonomy, absolutely.

I mean, she even consoles the addressee for not seizing her offer of total submission fast enough, "You ain't gotta worry / it's an open invitation."

There's a trace of self-love I guess in how she tacitly praises her own capacity for dispossession, but is that a brag?

It's a waiting that stakes itself on never being terminated by coming and getting it.

On the other hand, the strange dynamic economy of *Come And Get It* is such that while autonomy is handed over by the female singer to the object of her affection, there's also immanent confidence, that the songs says "When you're ready come and get it" not "If you're ever ready you can come and get it," there is no doubt it will eventually be come after and gotten.

Selena Gomez seems really nice.

A couple of months ago I went to see Dodie and Stephen read at the library.

The third reader was Alejandro Murguia, the poet laureate of San Francisco.

I had never seen him or read anything by him so I had a sort of open mind about it, but his reading was pretty meh.

The worst part of it was when he went on a brief rant about Selena Gomez, comparing her unfavorably with the "first Selena," Selena Quintanilla-Perez, who was murdered by the president of her fan club in 1995.

Both Selenas are from Texas, and the later Selena is named after the earlier Selena, who also seemed like a pretty nice person.

It's so weird that Selena was murdered by the president of her fan club, ostensibly her biggest fan.

Fuck it makes me mad when people ruin adoration.

The fan is the person who means it most when they say *continuez!* or should be.

Murguia's dismissal of Selena Gomez was passionate and bizarre.

Kevin said it gave him the creeps.

Stephen read a piece from his novel *Parasite* about attending a reading, in the very room in which we all sat, about how that performance had been the prompt for the writing he read, that and a little bit of crack.

Deep in the cartilage of this poem, its bumping, yelping, crack-smoking heart, is *Come And Get It* by Selena Gomez.

Selena Gomez's fans are known as "Selenators."

I don't know if there's an official club, and there is probably not a "head Selenator," but do you think Selena Gomez is worried about some Selenator going awry and murdering her?

I'm taking the *19 Signs You Might Be A Selenator* quiz on-line.

There are actually quite a few signs that I qualify as a Selenator, but three apply with certainty.

I understand the power of friendship.

I have an artistic side.

And most importantly, I understand that Selena Gomez is, like, superhuman.

When you feel home-ly love for someone, their continuance becomes nourishment, their absence the thirst of someone used to water.

I would wait bare butt on a glacier for those people who drive me wild with adoration, those for whom I am a mad and stubborn Selenator.

Tor Hermansen and Mikkel Eriksen wrote *Come and Get It* for Rihanna, but I'm glad Selena Gomez gets to sing those na na nan as.

The older Selena agrees with me, I know, in the halls of Hell or Valhalla or wherever she ended up.

TAYLOR SWIFT ft. ED SHEERAN, *EVERYTHING HAS CHANGED*

The first thing you hear on *Everything Has Changed* is Ed Sheeran's voice asking Taylor Swift, "Are you good to go?"

It's tender, of course, as is everything these two do together.

Sheeran is the Brit ginge male version of Taylor, an autodidact philosopher of love and emotion whose thought is grounded in manicured innocence, like he probably comes from some town with "-shire" in the name.

But the sound of his voice is also a spellbreak.

It's the first time we have evidence of the singers' bodies in the studio.

I remember as a kid I thought that when a song was played on the radio the singer and band actually played it live in the radio station.

So I guess the extended fantasy was that to be a singer was to live a transient and frenetic existence, caravanning between stations to play your hit before the next band came on to play theirs.

The real story about how the radio works is much weirder, is supernatural.

Everything Has Changed is a selfie aubade recognizing a reorganized contingency of feelings.

It's set in the moments after the singer wakes, reflecting on an eighteen hour period in which everything feels like it has changed.

The first thing I did this morning was put my glasses on and see if there was a BART strike.

Actually, the *first* thing I did was sit for a minute with my eyes closed, listening intently out the window, to see if I could "hear" whether there was a BART strike or not.

I went to sleep considering the adaptations I'd have to make to my own grievous moving aubade in case of a strike.

56

The sky in the morning is rapidly darker every day, you can really sense that everything is changing.

There was not a BART strike, but there had been earthquakes overnight, I didn't feel them.

We say we "sleep on" a cultural artifact when we fail to attend to it in the moment of its first thrumming entrance into the world, wince later at our stupid ability to have lived however long in a world without it.

It's freaky to sleep through earthquakes.

The structure of the Top 40 is not seismically safe, it cannot survive unagitated longer than one week.

Taylor's theme in *Everything Has Changed* is similar, the new and mysterious beloved has been an earthquake to the supposedly sound geological structures underpinning her body and her great poems.

Almost nothing happens in this legendary encounter.

All that can be said, in fact, is that the addressee introduced him or herself, names were exchanged, a door was held open for Taylor to walk in or out of.

But the stakes with Taylor are, as always, extremely high.

When she sings, "Your eyes look like coming home," she means the love that is *oikeios*, home-ly, no matter how new their acquaintance.

And thus when she sings "I feel like I've missed you all this time," she means that the object of this love feels like a lost possession, its absence retrospectively intolerable.

Taylor, perhaps more than anyone since Wordsworth, has famous powers of almost immediate reflective tranquility, although she is much less hysterical than Wordsworth.

Another proverbial idea of friendship is that it takes time to develop, and Taylor's no fool, she sings with impassioned caution, "I just wanna know you better / know you better / know you better."

Aristotle writes of the proverbial idea in Greece, that two friends can't call themselves friends until they've eaten a bushel of salt together.

It sounds like a lot of salt, but you get the idea.

The true friendship, the home-ly friendship, transforms temporality absolutely.

As a transit strike defamiliarizes the commuter.

A transit strike can be breathtaking actually in how it redistributes the possible.

Although it is annoying to wake up thinking about a commute and not the marvelous dream in which (redacted) (sorry) and I rubbed each other's cracks, stargazing in each other's eyes, our sex upset by the call to work.

Earthquake dreams, I guess.

Pop excels at narrating catastrophes like earthquakes, death, and meeting someone you instantly love, the events that bring about the feeling that everything has suddenly changed.

It's less good at judgment and strategy, sorry.

Ed Sheeran is from a place called West Yorkshire, but was raised in Framlingham, which was voted "Best place to live in the United Kingdom" in a 2006 *Country Life* poll.

I told you about the "-shire" thing!

I went into the living room towards everything I wanted to know better.

The rumbling liquid, a BART train, I couldn't hear a thing.

PARAMORE, *STILL INTO YOU*

Today I saw the word "mercy" three times.

The first was a cover of Brian Wilson's "Love and Mercy" that Dana posted, the second spread across a sweatshirt MERCY HIGH, the third after picking up Alice Notley's *Culture of One* on my lunch break and opening the book to the poem "The Mercy Moment."

She writes, "The world isn't a text to be deciphered, it is a new creation through ancient—but what is antiquity to me?

Every moment must destroy suffering anew; a cloud enters you, to begin in."

I don't think the world is a text to be deciphered either, but I do try to notice as much as possible when the present trumpets signs, today it was mercy.

"Mercy" feels so good as a thing to ask for or possess but it derives from all the words in Latin that start with *merc*—like *mercedes*, not a sweet car, but the word for wages, *merc* means a "commodity.""

Think "market," "mercantile," etc.

It's also related to *merci*.

I am so grateful to those who have made me feel like Hayley Williams singing *Still Into You*.

One of the things I love most about *Still Into You,* and there are a lot of things to love about it, is how it too is more or less an extension of a song I've listened to since I was a teenager, with subtle but powerful innovations.

If you think I'm alluding to Adorno's idea that a "pop hit" must have one feature which distinguishes it from the totality of other pop hits, well I'm fucking not!

The way it "destroys suffering anew," the way it becomes a cloud, is by construing a chorus not quite like any other ever, a baby with denture breath.

Hearing it I feel lepidopteral.

Still Into You begins with a faint but growing rumbling sound, the aural warning of an earthquake you can hear before you feel it.

Alli has been underwhelmed by it, mysteriously allergic to its melodic discovery and Hayley Williams' voice, which sustains and then spikes like the long wingspan of a starved raptor who suddenly smells a skunk corpse.

Part of her ambivalence is a dissatisfaction with the central assertion of the song, that the singer is still into you.

"That's not saying very much," she argues.

But I dunno.

I think the moment of "being-into" might be contrasted with the long resigned aeon of "being-with."

Its luster is usually tempered by brevity, but in this particular case being-into has lasted years in excess of its expected expiration.

I should be over the treasure heap of mercy this song summons through my ossicles and submit to all that wants to gall.

The temporal economy of the proletariat is real, there actually is only so much time, and I have decided to spend a good deal of it listening to *Still Into You* over, and over, and over again.

You know that NA vicissitude that "The definition of insanity is doing the same thing over and over again?"

If that's true, the record of how many times I've listened to this song with the exact same results is enough to qualify me as "insane."

If not listening to *Still Into You* is sanity, then I don't want to be sane.

Over the summer my sisters visited Oakland.

After a long night at the bar, Alli dropped me off and instead of going to bed I had a nightcap glass of Chardonnay, even though my sister told me that same Chardonnay had given her a stomach ache.

On the walk to the train the next morning, I felt a foreboding rumble in my guts, like the first seconds of *Still Into You*.

I tried to fool my body with a book, but the words started swimming, shit swelling at the outer lips, where my colon kisses air.

It became, uh, urgent.

I had a gorgeous outfit on, I was still into you, I was going to have exhaustive diarrhea on BART.

I imagined the faces of the commuters in the cramped car, liquid shit pooling out of the bottom of my trousers, the smell that would first rise and then spread, their screams and looks of horror and indignation.

I sympathized with them, I'd do the same thing if I were them.

And omigod, I really wished I were them and not me!

But I made it to the Hilton at the Embarcadero, fleeing the train and bounding up the stairs, past a conference table full of women wearing shirts that read "Don't Sweat the Cloud," I collapsed on plastic bowl, almost crying with relief.

When I got back on the train, late for work but feeling blessed, I forgot the book and listened to *Still Into You*.

Across from me this guy was looking at me intently.

He held a small hatchet in his lap, the kind you'd use to chop medium branches of a tree.

Whatever, I bobbed my neck in time with Hayley's leaps and dips said a silent *merci* to God for all the mercy I had seen.

PHILLIP PHILLIPS, *GONE, GONE, GONE*

Phillip Phillips, shit.

No wonder he ends up writing songs with repeating words in their titles, although one might think he'd be exhausted by repetition after a life of saying and hearing "Phillip Phillips."

I played *Gone, Gone, Gone* for Alli and asked her to guess what the singer's name was.

Her guess was "Shane Blake," pretty close.

Names aren't supposed to determine vocation.

But then you think of a poet named "Wordsworth," or you know how like every quarterback has a name like "Jake Locker."

It's like Phillip Phillips was named, if not born, to live his life in pop music, a form which loves repetition, reuse, recycling.

Gone, Gone, Gone starts by expressing the unconditional nature of the singer's love.

But then he demands reciprocity.

It's unclear what kind of love he wants finally, but clear that he does want it to not be gone.

I've started hearing each "Gone" as referring to successive degrees of absence, from the temporary lack of physical presence, to the abandonment of the love relationship, to the death of the lover.

When I think of the dead I've loved the feeling is thick, wet tea.

The presence of the beloved in the proximity of the lover is represented as song itself, "Like a drum baby, don't stop beating."

Proximity is the "beat" I guess.

Last night at dinner D.L. told us that at a recent artist residency in New York, the residency's directors asked him if there was anybody he'd like to meet while in New York, they'd try to arrange it.

It led to a parlor game for the table, who would you want to meet if you were D.L. and had this residency?

The game was fun and full of information.

Like most great parlor games, we used the question as a foil to tell our lives' stories to each other.

Pretty much all the names people said were singers.

Tim said "Lou Reed" but immediately looked disgusted and apologized for how trite he thought his answer was, this made me laugh.

Not his answer, his self-disgust.

I didn't really play honestly, because no one would get that the person I most wanted to meet in New York was Dana at Fitzgerald's, a disastrous tavern around the corner from the Carlton Arms, where we'd drink and talk for a couple hours before finding all of our friends before whatever.

Phillip Phillips suffers from a congenital kidney disorder which causes him to produce stones so big he cannot pass them.

I guess those stones have contributed to a lithological leitmotif for his entire existence, that's why his voice is so "gravelly."

When he won *American Idol* he had the stones removed with his winnings.

Do you know that when you win *American Idol* you have a "coronation?"

I think this will be great for his art, because if he's anything like me, ailments are even worse enemies of art than desperate poverty, and poverty is *very* bad for it.

Some say that long discussions of life "after the revolution" is a vital kind of parlor game, a "fuck marry kill" of politics.

But I dunno.

I guess that's a way to tell the story of your life, by describing what you will do with your winnings.

To dream elaborately out loud, to tell everyone you can about this dream, to hunt down Phillip Phillips and tell him about it.

In the dream you and he make an airport bar wet, if indeed they have airport bars and tears after the revolution.

Last time I moved, I found a bunch of old notebooks.

They were notebooks I kept in the early 90's, when I started writing poems.

I was a prolific juvenile, almost any feeling became the occasion for poetic activity, I could exaggerate the most minor mood shift into the language of evental myth.

In other words, not much has changed.

One of the poems I found was this ridiculous pseudo-*Season in Hell* thing, inspired I guess by the part where Rimbaud laments the bloody ontogenesis of the French "race."

My poem was about my supposed "Scandinavian ancestry," where I described myself "allegorically" as a Viking with a conscience, wishing I could slough off the insanity of the human male but alas "My hair is / the blonde mop of Norway / unruly and cold."

Thus pushing genetic immanence to extremes of its own already-bad logic, Jake Locker style, Phillip Phillipsesque.

I'm not even blonde, wtf!

ENRIQUE IGLESIAS, *TURN THE NIGHT UP*

Kathy Acker writes, "The only reaction against an unbearable society is equally unbearable nonsense."

I started thinking that Enrique Iglesias also knew this line of Acker's and it was his inspiration for *Turn The Night Up*.

Iglesias himself narrates the etiology of the song by describing a domestic scene, in which he walks through his manor, requesting a share of what anyone happens to be enjoying with the words, "Gimme some of that."

His girlfriend wipes peanut butter on a long celery slice, suddenly he appears, upbraiding her with those four little shitty words no one wants to hear.

"Gimme some of that."

What makes *Turn The Night Up*, if not unbearable, at least unpleasant as an object of listening, is that it's not quite a "song," rather a collage of various kinds of aural panic that never harmonize.

Like the soundtrack to a Tiqqun video game.

Its signs are bellicose but disembodied, its wails inhuman notes of ecstasy or fear, its landscapes two dimensional and abstract.

Its imperatives can't really be considered communicative, but the howls and barks sound like civil war.

Like the present was the present of a soft civil war, an unbearably soft civil war.

I content myself with the undeniable thought that for at least one person on earth *Turn The Night Up* has given their life sudden meaning.

For a while, it did feel like my friends were fighting a war.

At parties they would strip and show their wounds, the room would wince and cringe, you could tell the night was turning up.

And then a lot of the songs they would sing, and poems they would write, the story of their lives they would tell, became songs and poems and stories about violence.

It made me wonder.

At the time I thought it was strange for so many poets to so casually fantasize about violence.

I don't mean the unbearable quotidian violence of daily life that stems from global imperatives to produce for wage and reproduce for free, the basic and daily war against the global majority that is the reason we are all of us sick.

I mean like the kind of violence that has machetes or acts like machetes are good.

Of course, they were being hunted by aggressive psychos; later, they would talk about "stringing people (capitalists) up," slitting throats in Oscar Grant Plaza, they would laugh about a server smashed in the face with a brick during a demonstration.

I read a historical precedent for the violent poet, *Egil's Saga,* do you know this story?

Egil is a depraved brute, even lil mini Vikings on the play-fjord knew that.

But he was also a poet.

Most of his poems are metrical brags about the various people he's brutally murdered.

"I have wielded a blood stained sword / and howling spear; the bird / of carrion followed me / when the Vikings pressed forth."

Some say Hel is one long night with no morning.

Some say Enrique Iglesias is there, on a long residency, singing *Turn The Night Up* with no bridge and no coda, no end to the tweaky pitch it will reach.

The desolation of *Turn The Night Up*'s text is in contrast to the soundtrack of its eschatology, a rising tide of darkness louder and louder still.

I can't even go to the movies.

Representations of violence and gore are too traumatic, I watch with my fingers spread over my eyes the whole time, electing to deny the imagery on screen.

If I had my way, every film would be a stoner odyssey with a not-so-subtle anarchist subplot, but that is not our world I guess.

What's weird is I was better at watching violent imagery as a kid, I guess before too many of my friends died.

I know violence is bigger than the ways in which I'm using it in this poem, there doesn't have to be a raven licking blood off its beak over the splayed-out corpse of a dead Dane or psycho pigs in Oakland or a bunch of machetes or whatever.

I've tried to listen to *Turn The Night Up* a dozen times.

The form of covering the eyes for detrimental sound is, what, plugging ears up with pinkies?

The real irony would be if *Turn The Night Up* was Enrique Iglesias's way of announcing that he was a god and his divine power was that he could make lulling darkness loud as a growling puma.

It's October, the creepiest month to walk around after dark.

Easy to believe that some puma or armed poet lurks in fell foliage, waiting for you to walk by so it can rip up the sinews of your heart.

In *Egil's Saga,* the poet parties are full of ale and vomit, they too include spectacular violence.

Prosody, bandages, mead.

At the end of the night everything goes into the bonfire.

Those are nights you wouldn't turn up, unless you wanted to end up buried under a mound of rocks at daybreak.

JUSTIN TIMBERLAKE, *MIRRORS*

Do you know that Lefty Frizzell song *I Never Go Around Mirrors,* that's one of my favorites.

I spend a lot of time looking in bathroom mirrors, but not other kinds of mirrors, what's wrong with me?

Am I always in the bathroom?

Yesterday I went into the bathroom at work to pee.

A guy was at the urinal holding a big pile of newspapers and a cane.

We both washed our hands at the same time and the guy turned to me and said, "When I was young I never thought that it would be such an ordeal to take a piss."

I didn't know what to say to that, so I said "Yeah."

When he left the bathroom I regarded myself in the mirror for a while, first in profile, then full frontal, and I'll admit I had the "crazy" thought that maybe the guy who had been there was my older self who had traveled back in time, to deliver that message, a sort of mictural *memento mori.*

For a long time I thought Justin Timberlake sang, "With your hand in my hand / and a pocket full of *salt* / I can tell you there's no place we couldn't go."

It turns out it's "soul" not "salt," although arguably it's easier to visualize a pocket full of salt than a pocket full of soul.

There's a conventional model of friendship which says the friend is someone like oneself, and friendship is the attraction of like to like.

But how literally are we supposed to take Timberlake in *Mirrors*?

In the logic of *Mirrors,* you "Put two reflections into one," alterity disappears, one's image is swallowed by the singer's.

And while it might tempt you to think that is a sweet sentiment, the erasure of the beloved and his or her replacement by a reflection could also be thought of as the most extravagant narcissism.

Like if I'm the beloved in *Mirrors* I might be all, go make somebody else your mirror.

It feels too creepy to take *Mirrors* literally, so I've started thinking about it not as a love song for Jessica Biel, inspired by Timberlake's grandparents, but rather as a song addressed to pop music itself.

Pop, then, is the mutable reflective surface which both changes and changes with whoever gazes into it.

Some say pop precisely fails to reflect the miserable conditions of the real world, is instead a collection of highly addictive distractions, candied loops that desensitize its adherents to the stifling devastation of the world pop traffics in and which it helps to make.

They deduce from this thought that the popwork is an unsuitable political object, debilitating to the present imperatives of resistance.

But I dunno.

People really love to sing together, voices variously blended and distinct.

Poetry has always hearkened to a rhythmic demand that produces unmanageable excess, images too big to fit a sheet of molded glass or hustling hexameter.

When I look in the mirror I'm subject to a number of fantasies about history and time travel.

I try to locate my face as a younger person and fantasize about my face as an older person.

I'm a little worried about the structural integrity of my nasal capillaries, etc.

One of my least favorite experiences at the mirror is getting caught by somebody else barging into the bathroom.

I know they know what I'm up to.

I never feel more alone, it's the opposite of singing together.

Fred Moten and Stefano Harney write about the undercommons, as a place where fugitives gather from bad debt.

They gather although they always remain "on the run."

They write, "Having looked for politics in order to avoid it, we move next to each other, so we can be beside ourselves, because we like the nightlife which ain't no good life."

See, Justin Timberlake, this is another way!

To move in adjacency to one another, to enter into one another's shadow, to lie beside another or sit beside another, this can be dispossession from a long and deep, a common trance, it doesn't have to "just" be a series of mirroral reflections.

It's obvious that hanging out is ethical, especially over a big bushel of salt, slowly depleting.

I was just kidding earlier.

I know that Justin Timberlake doesn't mean that when he regards his beloved he only sees his own image.

What he means is, "I want you to continue, and perhaps, if I am capable of a radical fidelity to song, there may be a way for us to continue together, in renewable and continuing proximity."

The strings extend out into space and look back on the earth and then they are just the earth in tone.

Everyday time travel.

Everyday time travel, you are the love of my life.

ONE DIRECTION, *BEST SONG EVER*

Keston Sutherland writes, "Our tribute to the world is our desire, nothing else."

But desire is a tricky tribute, in that it always potentially goes rogue and tries to destroy the object it's supposed to apprehend.

The tribute is exacted from us by the world I guess, which constantly asks us to decide what we want and then eat it.

If I want to nibble the plastic rims of dirty diapers, this world will sell it to me.

There will always be an app for this, like that parlor proverb about pornography, you know, "If you can think of it, there will be a pornography for it," which is why money and pornography are similarly structured dystopias.

The guys in One Direction are British, just like Keston.

I have the intuitive sense, it is utterly uncorroborated, that One Direction has an entirely different meaning if you're British, like if you're USAmerican you have "feelings" about Elvis Presley no matter who you are.

I always think of how Merle Haggard says, "We loved Elvis to death," how sad that is.

Best Song Ever tells the story of a romantic encounter temporally bound by the confines of one long night, the soundtrack of which was one ostensibly very long song, you guessed it, the "best song ever."

As if the night itself were a pop song, ephemeral, unpossessible, but, paradoxically, as such eternal, brilliantly distributed and available for all to share.

The momentary eternal sounds like heaven to me.

In *This Is The End* (2013, dir. Evan Goldberg and Seth Rogen), Jay Baruchel and Seth Rogen are saved at the last minute from an eternity in the lake of fire and brought up to heaven in a blue beam of light.

Some of their friends are there, have already been there, know the ropes.

They learn that heaven is the place where what you wish for comes immediately true.

Jay wishes to see the Backstreet Boys, the 1990's version of One Direction, and immediately they appear, all of heaven starts to bob.

You might be tempted to read "best" in *Best Song Ever* as a reference to the sort of ranking and counting of which the Top 40 is the apotheosis, but no.

Instead, the "best song ever" turns out to only survive as choral melodic fragments, "woah oh oh" and "yeah yeah yeah," onomatopoetic signifiers of togetherness and bliss.

The best song ever constitutes a paralinguistic place beyond where words mean, the guys in One Direction traveled to this realm that night, and it was there they experienced a protopop that was also an uberpop, an *apokalypsis* in the literal sense, that as the strappings of any particular song were stripped away, the evidence was revelatory.

A revelation, critically, that the singer can no longer remember.

Like imagine if Dante had woken up and thought "best katabasis ever" but never written about the terrace of the gluttons or the fifth sphere of heavenly warriors, what would our books look like then?

People really love to dance together.

At Woolsey this summer one dance party outdid itself.

Outside, I draped over the porch panting, I thought "best gym ever."

I suppose the risk of stating the superlative is that the superlative risks dissolution the moment it coheres, that bestness always invites competition.

Perhaps that is the genius of *Best Song Ever*, which constantly deprives the object of the "best" any material trace or form.

The best dance party I have ever been to was at Private Line in March, after Brandon, Dana, and Clark read.

I hardly remember anything about it, which like the song in *Best Song Ever* is a proof of how pudding it was.

Singing with Ben and Monica and Jenny, the song was like woah oh oh.

People really love to dance and sing together.

I think the song we sang was like yeah yeah yeah.

It would be useful to imagine a way in which our desire could be a tribute to the world that didn't shave meat off the slender bones in us.

That it too could be melodic fragments, forgettable or not, we'd relish our tribute, it would harmonize eventually.

There are two moments in *Best Song Ever* where the singer tries to possess what he cannot.

When he asks Georgia Rose for his dispossessed heart back she says "Never in your wildest dreams."

When he asks Georgia Rose if he can take her home, presumably to be groped, she says "Never in your wildest dreams."

It's sad to think of dreams that aren't wild, wallflower dreams too shy to blend sweat.

I read something sad today on the Internet.

Friends described themselves as "Enemies of the dream."

I guess if our tribute to the world is our desire, then doesn't that include our dreams, don't we all want to love our dreams, aren't they the same thing as our thoughts?

LADY GAGA, *APPLAUSE*

Applause is both a love song to Lady Gaga's own glory and an ersatz love song on behalf of pop music sung addressed to us.

For in *Applause,* Gaga becomes a metonym for all pop when she recognizes that the enduring life of her efforts depends on our willingness to absorb, be moved by, and reiterate her work.

She needs us to ensure that her deeds not only shine in the interior penumbral of our own solar system, but also echo in far off moons and coteries of moons.

Kings in ancient Iceland welcomed berserk killers like Egil to their cribs because they knew how endless his art would try to make them.

It's not like it was very much fun to be around them.

In *Applause,* Gaga describes this desire for enduring fame as a craving.

Her dream of fame is that it could be administered intravenously.

But there would be something missing in that case, right?

Puncture pain.

The rising sound of hands touching each other, impelled by reciprocating affirmation.

All addicts say something like this about their drugs of choice.

Like a tired person will tap his or her veins and indicate coffee, we get it, it's an Esperanto all craven druggies know.

Lou Reed died on Alli's birthday, it sucked.

We had a perfect day together, applauding Alli's continued existence, a daylong homage to sensory fulfilments, known and unknown, possible and impossible.

Lou Reed dying was the opposite of how Gaga sings in *Applause,* "Give me the thing that I love," it was the thing I hated most.

When a singer dies, it's the worst.

When a king dies, rule does hardly, backs still bend under a different set of gilded Docs the moment his shitty lungs elapse.

I guess when a king dies some people are even cheered, maybe even moved to applaud.

Fuck a king, but even a king's death is not as good as the dumbest pop song.

When a singer dies, the whole world droops.

Justin said he didn't often think people would live forever but that Lou Reed had warranted that feeling in him, that the world he knew, in sum, was a world that contained Reed, this new one, we didn't know; it seemed suckier.

The daylight shores up at the world's end, life continues in weakened light, basketball season starts, it finally becomes sweater weather.

After Alli's birthday, I went on a boozy and druggy vacation, it was so good.

On my vacation, wherever I went, drunk and high and in between being drunk and high, I heard Lou Reed's voice everywhere.

Maybe the right way of saying what it was like to think he would never die is to simply say that his presence in this world was addictive.

I punctuated endless rounds of drinks with crumbs of speed to dilate hanging out as much as possible.

This was important because I will always be poor and the hours I spend with my friends are pearls thereby, for that little longer I'll always be grateful.

I was of course immediately addicted, and although I kicked quick, everything for a couple of days took on the desperate drag of missing dopamine.

I guess in retrospect Tim's desire to meet Lou Reed of all possible New Yorkers became drastically less trite.

To do it now would demand more than a plane ticket to New York.

The drug Lady Gaga craves in *Applause* is a feeling contingent on Gaga having transcended the human, our pathetic and slavish satisfaction with merely feeling okay.

I remember hearing *Heroin* for the first time, it was like watching a tragedy in the future.

But whereas *Heroin* suggests the arrival of glorious opiate okayness by the thickening pace and depth of its noise, *Applause* literally embeds what it begs for.

But it is finally a work of difference, and "Give me the thing that I love" is a pure imperative, the imperative's solo commanding voice, lonesome finally.

Applause reminds me of ancient Roman comedy.

In Alison Sharrock's *Reading Roman Comedy*, she writes, "Applause is not a spontaneous response of pleasure and appreciation.

It is a ritualized convention which itself plays a part in the act of performance.

Roman comedy had a very simple way of telling the audience 'that's all folks!'"

An actor says directly to the audience, *plaudite*, "clap now," always in the imperative.

AVICII, *WAKE ME UP!*

I'm on the wagon this week after my boozy and druggy vacation.

Nights when I'm on the wagon I often take a melatonin to sleep, not because I can't sleep if I'm on the wagon but I have this nagging fear that I won't be able to sleep, and then it will be too late to take the melatonin, which I don't actually *know,* but I *fear* that if I take the melatonin too late I won't be able to wake up, and this subjunctive insomnia overwhelms any native resistance I might have to pharmaceuticalizing somnolescence, so I just take one most of the time.

Melatonin is famous for giving users vivid dreams, and I've been having them, bad ones I'd yell inside of if I could *wake me up!*

In humans, melatonin is a hormone produced by the pineal gland, an endocrine gland the size of a pea, lodged in the middle of the brain.

I know this is really stupid, but for a while I had somehow conceived the notion that melatonin was a hormone produced...
by the sun.

And that the reason taking melatonin made you so tired is that it quickly replicated the effect of being in the sun for too long.

Fuck, I know.

But why should I know anything?

Everything I've ever learned has been scrapped together from the lot behind regular schools, in the narcotic and hyperhedonic halls of song and metrics, cottage doctorate.

I was really confused by *Wake Me Up!* the first few times I heard it.

The confusing thing was the seeming incommensurability of the song's two sections, the baritone grit of the verses versus the jig-a-jig bright house parts that bridge them.

The mix is reflected in the collaboration of Sweden's Avicii and

USAmerica's Aloe Blacc, they meet on *Wake Me Up!*'s international waters.

What the song can't conflate it arranges side by side like, uh…the zoo?

The bright dancey part whinnies next to the Baudelairean worship of nothingness in Aloe Blacc's lyrics.

Although I can see Avicii having his dark side too.

I felt so superior to him for having named himself that, that little extra "i" the crowning disachievement of his entire project.

But yet again I find myself inflated, popped, then pupping up later.

To the Internet, and Avicii, all three little i's in his name.

"In Buddhism it means the lowest level of hell," he says of his DJ name.

"I was honestly just looking for a MySpace name and had remembered the word Avicii from a friend.

It just sounded cool," he adds.

As he would have learned as a child in Sweden, the lowest level of hell in Norse mythology is Hel, the ninth of the Nine worlds, a grim and high hall, where Odin rides, where Baldr went without suffering death, below the roots of the world tree Yggdrasil.

I've listened to *Wake Me Up!* dozens of times; at first I felt a little resentful of its theses.

Like when he sings, "Wish that I could stay forever this young…" with such pathos, like I'm supposed to feel sorry for him for being *young,* please.

But now I dunno.

I've started thinking about the song as a sincere expression of a desire for the negativity of sleep, the utopian yearning for long oneiric repose.

And thus, upon waking, one really would be "older and wiser," schooled by dreamy pedagogues.

I'd *love* to blame that idiotic theory I had about melatonin on a vivid dream or youth, but nope.

Wake Me Up! is the only song in America's Top 40 with an exclamation point, which accentuates the imperative with urgency.

There's also something sort of apocalyptic about it, right?

"Wake me up when it's all over" suggests a disinclination to witness firsthand the eradication of the world, even at the risk of punctuated enervation.

And there really is a fitless sense of despair when Aloe sings, "Hope I get the chance to travel the world / but I don't have any plans."

It's the perfect expression of the iconic young unemployable European, bred into a culture founded on individualism and exploration; disastrous as this has been for the history of the world (very), the circumstances which now forbid it are lamentable also.

The Norse apocalypse known as Ragnarok is heralded by the crowing of a sooty-red cock from the halls of Hel.

After Ragnarok, there are only two humans left living on earth.

Maybe that's one of the concealed meanings of this collaboration between Avicii and Aloe Blacc, like it'll be the two of them.

They'll be older, wiser, alive, etc.

I think of all the times I've woken up to experience a soft apocalypse.

A soft, dehydrated apocalypse.

A lot of those times I would have done anything to be able to go back to sleep.

MACKLEMORE AND RYAN LEWIS,
CAN'T HOLD US

In *Back To The Future* (1985, dir. Robert Zemeckis), Marty McFly travels back thirty years into the past.

After a series of hijinks, he is forced to arrange that his real life parents fall in love at the school dance.

If he fails, they will not fall in love, never fuck, he will never exist in the future.

For a while, things do not go well, and Marty, already quite pale in all his limbs and features, starts to literally disappear in this artificial present.

As Marty's body begins to disintegrate, his dissolving hand can't strum the bright chords of the guitar, giving off transparent grape vapor.

This disappearance takes place at a very inopportune time, as he has agreed to play guitar for the band playing the prom.

The band's leader is named Marvin Berry, ostensibly, as we learn, Chuck Berry's cousin.

The ensemble sounds worse and worse with Marty in Marvin's place.

Ultimately it works out, his parents kiss, their falling in love is assured, Marty's hand is restored, and he then plays a song of his "own."

The song is *Johnny B. Goode*, a song written in real life by Chuck Berry in 1955.

Johnny B. Goode is a rock'n'roll song about a "Poor country boy who plays a guitar just like ringing a bell," although Berry substituted "country boy" for "colored boy" before the song was released, understanding that racist white people might be disinclined to celebrate a song whose protagonist was black.

In the film, while Marty goes needlessly Van Halen on *Johnny*, the camera shows Marvin Berry calling "his cousin Chuck."

"You know that new sound you've been looking for?" he asks.

Holding the phone out towards the stage, he commands cousin Chuck, 'Listen to *this!*'

The irony is obviously as big and strong as a Jötunn.

Many people hear *Johnny B. Goode* for the first time watching *Back To The Future*.

Macklemore's *Can't Hold Us* is Poundian almost in the breadth of its allusions to traditional hip hop tropes in the service of supporting his own fairly conventional claims to greatness as an artist.

Can't Hold Us alludes to, at least: Sir-Mix-A-Lot's *Posse on Broadway*, Kanye West's *Can't Tell Me Nothin'*, A Tribe Called Quest's *Can I Kick It?*, and the Wu-Tang Clan's periodontal sartorialism.

I'm not just taking a cheap shot at Macklemore.

I'm implicated in this totally, as you know by now.

I've said many times that I credit the early experience of nearly constant attention to certain rap songs with my becoming a poet.

You know how in *The Prelude,* Wordsworth rows a boat out onto a moonlit pond, awed by the susurrations of cattails in the lunar lit breeze and the poem latently suggests this experience was formative to his later development as a poet?

Well for me it was just like that, dragging a mower, churning up snipped grass, mosquitoes drinking my blood, flipping off my dad when he frowned at my careless lines in the grass, playing N.W.A.'s *Straight Outta Compton* over and over and over.

It wasn't just that Ice Cube's rage (which was, of course, vehemently about race and class) transposed easily onto the miasmatic feelings of resentment I felt in my white way.

That rage was delivered in the most outrageous metrical innovations.

When Ice Cube intones, "Íce Cúbe would líke to sáy / that I'm a crázy motherfúcker / from aroúnd the wáy," it is an exemplary instance of very regular measures surrounding quick tribrachs of hurtling syllables, broken up by the lightest stresses, light as a mosquito's proboscis.

In *Can't Hold Us,* the night is figured as a "moment."

But in this song, as in many other pop songs of the last few years, the night is less like a moment, in the conventional, kairotic sense of the moment as fleeting, and more like the recognizable and potentially long time of an agon.

In fact, the metaphor is frequently not just a confrontation but a war, "We'll fight til it's over."

I guess I'm not sure how you beat night.

The war doesn't end until someone wins, but does night always?

I suppose that *Can't Hold Us* would suggest that the boundaries of night be understood not solely as temporal, but also spatial or experiential, like the ceiling could be night, passing out could be night, whatever kind of lid there is must be absolutely challenge cracked.

The only allusion Macklemore makes to his own white skin is comparing himself to a shark.

Indeed, Macklemore and his friends call themselves the "Shark Face Gang," in the sense that a shark I guess is white?

Great White Sharks eat a lot, and almost anything, I guess.

I know after *Personism* the consensus on meter is that it's supposed to be obvious, like tight pants.

Although there's not a consensus about tight pants anymore either.

Just ask Macklemore, or I mean, look at him, or just ask Ice Cube, or actually don't, just wear your pants as tight as you mean to.

Apparently Chuck Berry said he thought the scene in *Back To The Future* is funny, but I wonder if he meant funny ha ha.

Now I know one thing I'd like to ask Chuck Berry if I ever get to meet him.

DAFT PUNK ft. PHARRELL WILLIAMS, *GET LUCKY*

Get Lucky starts with the "legend of the Phoenix," a story about the stubborn refusal of one creature to accept death—and by metonymy any imposition of an "end"—as final, preferring rather the circular idea that the end is the beginning.

The song appropriates the legend of that outstanding bird, the rising, the ash, in order to make a manifesto in praise of endurance and repetition.

Luck is pictured as a side effect of defying a smoldered eternity, to have your flourishing stubbed out by the sunrise, sunrise of the sky or sunrise of the spirit.

Get Lucky suggests that repetition is endurance's strategy.

Playing it over and over again in recent days it feels Phoenical, I'm brought back to nights this summer, how afternoon infected night properly speaking, *Get Lucky* a brilliant wind stirring your hair, you reach up to find your fingers glammed with glitter and ossified cocaine shards, deep October takes on aestival hues.

I guess I feel permission to wear my summer body around in the winter time thanks to *Get Lucky* because they're so candidly visiting the pink chic heaven of the 1970's in the song itself.

Even if you don't know who Nile Rodgers is, his guitar playing on *Get Lucky* sounds ancient, native, a kernel.

This summer at Woolsey, Jason put on *Get Lucky* and the two of us danced alone for a while before Sophie joined.

Without missing a move she shouted over the speakers, "This song is so fucking boring!"

But I dunno.

I think she was referring to the excessive repetition in the song's structure, bored by its stubborn refusal to do anything but stay up all night to get lucky.

Only two things happen, basically, and one of them is Pharrell and sometimes a robot singing the line "We're up all night to get lucky."

In fact he sings those words at least thirty six times.

One might say that Pharrell and these French spaceman producers doth defend too much what they do and how late they do it.

I hardly ever stay up all night, much more often I get up before night's even technically over.

Alli hates it when I leave in this liminal zone, she calls it "barbaric."

She's right of course, ironically this barbarism is the token of how civilized I have become.

As opposed to Pharrell and these two French guys.

In the morning I have the chance to appraise how people did in terms of getting lucky or not getting lucky.

A hypothesis for my research is that if you're still awake on 14th Street when I'm walking down it to go to work, the odds are overwhelmingly against you having gotten lucky.

Mostly people have gone to bed, so all the evidence I have of their luck is what they leave behind.

This morning I saw a pile of puke by the tattoo parlor, full of popcorn, like little burnt orange molars, tossed over trash cans, tears, the dead.

Daylight savings has made it "instant winter" as Amy put it, and all the more perverse to keep listening to *Get Lucky*, compulsively, obsessively, letting it persuade me to render the darkness hypothetical, I layer linens on in my mind, deimmobilizing summer.

At the end of my boozy and druggy vacation I spent a night in a casino, don't ask.

My dad loves to gamble, and loves for me to take a small amount of cash and gamble it promptly into nothingness.

I always consider breaking the bill on a few weak casino drinks before devising a sob story about losing it all, I waste it later on an airport appletini, my terminal frenemy.

But I always end up playing, some imp inside me wants to get lucky.

There is no more place more boring than a casino.

Walter Benjamin compares gambling to masturbation, but I dunno, masturbating isn't so boring.

Gambling is a premonition, an inkling, not of sex, something weirder.

When I was there I was still thinking about Lou Reed dying, and about addiction, like what is it, and I could see the structure of gambling addiction, how the players fabricated ornate systems of desire and reward, everything is counting.

I could see it because I know this structure intimately.

Cigarettes, drinks, pills, chips, fucks, syllables, reps, hours on the job, whatever it is, counting is addiction's constant praxis.

I shouldn't let this poem turn into a discursive substitute for a months-long argument I've been having in my head with Sophie about *Get Lucky* being boring or not.

For some reason I let it hurt *my* feelings, like she meant *I* was boring.

Ugh.

What I should have done instead is compare *Get Lucky* to a poetic form, it is in one after all, about counting and pattern, how counting and pattern war against boredom in form.

Like a sestina about how nagging the thought *I want to fuck you* can be.

You know, a "sextina."

Sorry.

JAY-Z ft. JUSTIN TIMBERLAKE, *HOLY GRAIL*

The other day Thom posted a link on Facebook with the words "Jay-Z Found Dead Inside" above a recent picture.

Suffering the momentary assumption that the link would provide a predicate for "inside", like "inside...his yacht" or "inside... Babies R Us," I felt a dropping pressure from my diaphragm into my intestines.

A sensation like hunger, but horrible, like a hunger for the flesh of infants.

I had just read Patti Smith's elegy for Lou Reed, she talked about the day of his death, October 27th, as the birthday of Sylvia Plath and Dylan Thomas, "the day of poets."

She left out Alli, Brian, and Susan, but still, it was too soon after this contemplation of funereal calendrics to consider admitting Jay-Z to the craggy pathways down to Hel or Valhalla or wherever he'll end up.

A few months ago I "volunteered" to work a mandatory work event.

I was taking coats from the rich and the demi-rich, hanging them on long aluminum shafts, tagging each like they were corpses, which some of them literally were.

Taking advantage of a tiny lull in "customers" I peeked at my phone, I had like ten texts.

They came from different friends, but all had the same message, "Lil Wayne is dying."

I felt how I felt when I read "Jay-Z Found Dead Inside", blurry but extreme fear, I frantically texted for more information in between hanging furs, grimaced to find even Snoop Dogg had tweeted with some *gravitas* about the imminent death of Wayne.

I had to say something so told a coworker, but prefaced by asking him, "Do you know who the rapper Lil Wayne is?"

He gave me this look like, "You know I live on the planet Earth, right?"

I deserved it I guess.

My phone couldn't be conclusive about Wayne living or dying by the time I left.

I traded all the coats for tags, then walked to the train somberly, unknotting my headphones to revisit the glorious work of Wayne's last decade.

On the train home, I decided that if Lil Wayne died, I'd know as soon as I crested the escalator stairs into Oscar Grant Plaza, where if I heard his music streaming out of phones and passing cars it would mean the worst had happened.

Lil Wayne didn't die that night, Jay-Z didn't die that day, the headline was a satire suggesting Jay's recent work was "lifeless," a shoe without toes.

It would make sense to assume that *Holy Grail* would refer to Jay's extraordinary capacity to purchase luxury commodities of transcendent value, lower limit Basquiats, upper limit Jesus silverware.

But no.

The grail in *Holy Grail* is actually held in the hands of the audience, the grail is pop itself, and this scenario shows that while ironically popworks are intended to secure immortal glory, this immortality can only manifest via consumers, slurping on the cup lip.

Jay-Z and Justin Timberlake seem sort of disappointed with us in this regard.

Our caprice, our carelessness, most of all our *spite* is what we exchange for their haloed products, when all we should be giving them is ceaseless love.

What's wrong with us?

As a kid I saw *Indiana Jones and the Last Crusade* (1989, dir. Steven Spielberg) a bunch of times.

It tells the story of an archaeologist whose father, also an archaeologist, has gone missing in search of the holy grail, the legendary cup Jesus used as a wine glass at the Last Supper.

I was obsessed with the idea of a hidden object that contained the power of immortality.

I read all the books I could find about the grail legend.

The God of the grail legends was the Christian God I liked.

Not the bored one thumbing harp, trimming beard in a field of singing weed, but the God who would occasionally pop down to earth to endow an object with magical powers, incinerate a rock with the words of the law, or put you inside a big ass fish for fun.

The one whose wrath was like a cloud.

I stopped believing in that kind of magic, and then I became a poet, and now I dunno.

Jay-Z doesn't strike me as the suicidal type, but he frames his disappointment with how our disappointing loyalty dampens his daily praxis by referencing Kurt Cobain, a strange fake threat.

Justin Timberlake sounds so sad about being famous in this song I am almost sympathetic.

I mean, I am a *little* sympathetic.

I wouldn't wish that kind of fame on my worst enemy, not even the person I'm "in hate" with.

That's one key difference between hate and love.

When I'm in love with someone, that means an enduring desire for their efflorescence, contagious photosynthesis, light with chasing leaking trunks of light.

So you might think that being in hate would effect the opposite feeling, the desire for the object of hate to fail and wither away.

But I dunno.

I would never want a singer to die, even a bad one, not the worst one ever.

JASON DERULO, *THE OTHER SIDE*

Today is David's birthday, thank God for David's continuance.

David shares a birthday with Saint Augustine and Whoopi Goldberg, all thoughtful Scorpios whose efforts have had moderate to great influence on the present work.

I quit smoking three days ago, it's so stupid.

One perverse tic that's emerged is that I've started drawing my right index and middle fingers to my lips, sucking in and inhaling air, returning it as if this mime could be satisfactory, it's weird and not.

Sara and David and I went to Ike's for sandwiches before Dodie's talk and I said feebly, "I'm only going to say this once…I *really* fucking want to smoke" and I did want to.

I forgot to buy David's sandwich as an anticipatory birthday gift, what's wrong with me?

This summer in Chico, I told my friends that I was going to quit smoking and David said, "That's good, because we love you."

I'm only quitting smoking because of a barely defensible belief in the future.

I mean that the future is whatever administrates our concupiscence in the present, and this is how Jason Derulo thinks about the future too.

Obviously I'm just going to replace my addiction to cigarettes with another addiction.

What do you think it should be?

Jason Derulo and I made a list of replacement addictions that we thought might not be so bad.

The list included exercise, studying paradigms for the pronoun in Old Norse, julienning kale, cunnilingus, practicing piano scales, "insane" facial and/or dental hygiene, letter-writing, and comprehensive dusting.

The Other Side is set in the moment before the singer makes a commitment to a permanently altered way of life.

It's all predicated on a new thought, a thought the singer thought he would never have, about going to the other side.

He needs a comrade in order to realize this metabolic adoption of new practice.

I understand that completely.

I was supposed to quit smoking a week before I did, after my boozy and druggy vacation, but Alli was out of town and to try and do it without her would have been a futile exercise ending in shame, failure, ashes sprinkled with tears.

In *The Other Side*, the singer's situation precipitated by new forms of cognizance brought about by devout sharing ("now you're eating off my spoon"); its initial symptoms are intoxication and property destruction.

I believe he believes it when he sings, "We're going all the way."

But I wonder how literally he means it when he sings that it's "Do or die."

The question of a dilemma between praxis and death is the literal meaning of what we say in English when we say, "X is at stake," the stake is that big long piece of vertical timber that English speakers traditionally bind women and the poor to and set on fire.

Which is the dark allusion of Jason Derulo singing, "Sparks fly / like the 4th of July," the American history of corpses.

Some of my friends are really interested in the question of "stakes," like what's "at stake" in writing poetry and in insurrectionary activity.

They freely describe art and poetry as "low stakes," as if some work warrants the question of life and death and some work does not so much.

Obviously this poem about Jason Derulo 's *The Other Side* is the Mauna Kea of high stakes poetry.

On the little drawing of Derulo on my device, his neck is rendered with a tattoo that reads "Tattoos."

This and the fact that he sometimes puts an umlaut in spelling his last name, *DeRülo,* are the two bases I can find for feeling just a little superior to him, he's obviously a god, and I'm an idiot.

Is the only way to go "all the way" to risk your life?

And if it is, how responsible should we be to answering for our lives?

For instance, what if the very real battles between us and the crazy cops are an inkling of a future war, harder and more literal than a rehearsal.

Would the loss of our lives now be worth it?

These are all real questions for me.

I know some of you are skeptical about that sly switch from "I" to "we," how I made a little us-ie in my poem, since I don't go out and fight the crazy cops myself.

And that's okay, you can be skeptical.

I'm skeptical too, and Jason Derulo is skeptical, and meanwhile we both quit smoking and sing as loudly as we can, our voices drowned out by the music but we read each other's lips and love what we read there.

Licking something sweet together off one common spoon, our tongues graze.

Every Sunday as a kid, listening to America's Top 40, wearing out thin lines of cassette tape, scraping grass off a lawn, in my room prostrate with headphones, in every scenario I was always alone.

So be easy on me if I exaggerate how gorgeous it feels to sing and dance with you now.

I want to keep doing it, all the way, but I don't want all the way to just mean death, I think of the *longue durée* of Jason Derulo, of life on the other side, of all the things we'll wear and do there, of the kiss that snaps like the flint of a lighter, a black lighter embossed with a pirate insignia, Oakland, life on this side even, the camaraderie of pure piracy, fifteen gasps, fifteen sucks, my loves.

JUSTIN TIMBERLAKE,
TAKE BACK THE NIGHT

Ernst Bloch writes about the worker at night, "Fresh air is taken in, alcohol washes down the dust."

I had fantasies about what it would be like to work when I was older, but one thing I never admitted into this fantasy was the extreme scarcity of free time.

I could have known, it was there for me to see.

My mother filled her few free hours a week with church commitments, commodity parties, and reining in the gross urges of four pasty blobs (I'm one of them!)

For my father, the long workday was followed by the long work night gambling on the riverboat, with only an hour in between to eat warmed monosodium glutamate and corn #2 with the rest of us.

I couldn't conceptually differentiate the hours occupied with the call of labor and the time when that call subsided.

I never knew how precious these hours would become.

Of course calling it "free time" is comic, ironic, it's the time when mostly what we do is spend money.

So many of the songs in America's Top 40 are obsessed with the night.

Not just the night as such, the time long obsessed over in the West, in which darkness permits previously impossible modes of privacy, freedom, perversions, but the night as a militarized opportunity which *must not be squandered.*

In other words, the proverbial *carpe diem* is more frequently found in pop as a *carpe noctem*, one literal way to translate Justin Timberlake's *Take Back The Night* into Latin.

Well, there is that "back" in "take back," so *recarpere noctem* I guess.

For a song whose rhetoric urges merciless retaliation, *Take Back The Night* sounds so chill.

Imagine pale, cold wine that *tasted* like the sound of flutes but *meant* destruction of sovereignty as we know it.

Thank you disco for being an electric blanket on a winter night in the freezing basement of the anthropocene.

Even as disco demands its listeners move, the moving it calls for is so groovy, narcotic, Pied Piper shit, luring all the town's kids into the club to squirm in unison until dawn.

But Timberlake recalls those bodies out onto the sidewalk, gestures towards the materials of night, sets them loose.

His utopian text ushers them into a nocturnal Gettysburg where they fight with moly bayonets.

It's hard to tell, in *Take Back The Night,* whether the central syntagm is a hortatory or an imperative.

On one hand, there's a clear and legible first person plural, "They're gonna try to shut us down / I'll be damned if we gon' let them."

But see how confusing that is, grammatically?

"*I'll* be damned if *we* gon' let them?"

As the number of the speaking voice in the song slips between the plural and the singular, the degree to which Justin Timberlake commands his addressee wanders from "let's go" to "come on."

Lenin writes famously, "Our task is not to champion the degrading of the revolutionary to the level of an amateur, but to *raise the amateurs to the level of revolutionaries.*"

In Timberlake's political economy, this is formulated as a hortatoric imperative to share his extraordinary vision and join him in a metaphorical armed revolt against *what or whoever* has "stolen" the night.

"Tonight's the night, come on surrender / I won't lead your love astray, astray, yeah / Your love's a weapon."

The problem for Timberlake, and I guess Lenin too, is pinpointing exactly who has taken away the night in the first place.

Because the night is the metabolic diamond of time, it is the jewel bosses covet.

Our obedience to bosses includes the way we rest our bodies.

Yesterday morning I was officially sick, although I was technically just tired, although is being so tired an ordinary way of being sick?

Alli and I slept in for most of the morning, a cruel metonymic luxury representing the free time enjoyed by the rulers of this world and those they permit to rest.

The extra two hours we slept in were like whole years in the life of Wordsworth, while he walked around Wales freaked out about the sudden appearance of a full moon on a leafy dale or whatever.

The whole day was permeated by 18th century laziness.

Because laziness is the sole residual fragment of paradise.

Because blue overhead, holiday feeling.

Alli took a long shower, and I listened to Black Uhuru's *Red*.

I thought about albums and poems and books named *Red,* and I wanted to write something and call it *Red*.

For everyone who is arraigned to hourly wage, or those who are arraigned to the demand of unwaged reproductive work in the interest of redeeming oneself from debt, knows that the only thing worse than being ill in general is to be ill during one's minuscule "free time."

We who are arraigned must find each other, even if the only light is glitterlight. SPACE We must find each other, and we must take back the night (and the day.)

BRUNO MARS, *TREASURE*

You might have heard there was some controversy about Justin Timberlake using the phrase "take back the night" for *Take Back The Night*.

"Take Back The Night" is the name of a solidarity march against rape and other forms of violence against women.

Timberlake himself claimed to have never heard of the "Take Back The Night" march.

It's weird to think about all the things that you know about that Justin Timberlake doesn't.

One of the mysteries of art is how young people who don't know about so many things remain capable of making great and wise artworks.

Bruno Mars too does not present the most sophisticated thoughts about gender, to say the least.

Treasure takes place in a robust scene of patriarchal prerogative and objectification, from its opening line, "Give me your attention baby," to its fundamental predication, that the object of his attraction is most properly expressed in monetary terms.

It's all address.

Mars sings, "Pretty girl, pretty girl, pretty girl, you should be smiling / A girl like you should never look so blue."

Alli tells me that men are always yelling at her in the street and telling her to smile.

This seems insane to me and it is of course insane.

I guess Bruno Mars has probably not read Gayle Rubin's *The Traffic In Women*.

Rubin writes, "If it is women who are being transacted, then it is the men who give and take them who are linked, the woman being a conduit of a relationship rather than a partner to it."

If he had only read these lines, who knows what *Treasure* would sound like?

But I can't put all of this on Bruno Mars; I'm not sure love is ever expressed in non-monetary terms except perhaps in flinches and grunts, oceanic and unutterable, once language comes around it blings.

I do of course wish that Bruno Mars would come to Oakland, and we could get him in a radical feminist reading group at the free school.

He probably thinks that *Treasure* is cotton candy 15th wave disco, simple, sweet and charitable.

I guess it's presumptuous to assume that the object of his song is a woman or even a human being instead of actual treasure?

Like maybe he's singing into the pulpy eyes of Ulysses S. Grant on a crisp fifty.

Once you start transforming everything into money, it's hard to stop.

Even desire, our tribute to the world, takes on handled copper smell.

Sometimes when I hear Bruno Mars's singing voice I think of Rod Stewart, the living instantiation of a chain-smoking feather.

There was an infomercial for a compilation of disco songs I saw like 10,000 times as a kid.

In the infomercial was a snippet of Rod Stewart's *Da Ya Think I'm Sexy?*

Sometimes those five seconds of *Da Ya Think I'm Sexy* seemed like the catchiest five seconds of pop music ever written.

Treasure.

I think about a concomitant world with this one, where feathers smoke, love is finally expressed lucrelessly, flawless nostrils ever-more, Bruno Mars and Silvia Federici collabo, all the grunts and flinches harmonize.

Part of me believes in pretending that that world obtains now, it does I guess, but only as light off shook foil.

Steve sent me a video where Lorde is talking about her song *Royals*.

She says that she actually did come up with the idea of using the word "royals" by seeing an image of George Brett, *ROYALS* in baby blue letters across his chest.

The craziest I get is when I think that this story is only true because of the poem I wrote about *Royals*.

The sanest is when I stand in front of an ATM and wait for money to come out of it.

I have $665.02 in my checking account, and $1.01 in my savings account.

I suppose part of the overall picture of treasure in my life is that I "possess" a large amount of debt, $49,855.15 today, some of that mystery debt laps the sides of the galaxy in which I walk around listening to *Treasure*.

The thought of this debt is good reason to publicly frown.

If you see me walking down the street with a frown I might just be thinking of that galactic fact.

Feel free to try and cheer me up, as being a cis man nobody is ever going to give me that old vulture face and command me to smile.

When I paid $1.99 to download *Treasure* I was given the option of the "explicit" or clean version.

From all I can tell, the only difference is that the "explicit" version has a brief intro, where a text-to-speech bot has been programmed to say "Baby squirrel, you's a sexy motherfucker."

If only *Treasure* was truly addressed to infant squirrels, and Bruno Mars was demanding they smile and consent to become his property.

Not that I have some kind of grudge against infant squirrels, but you have to admit it's a basically better world in which he does so.

KATY PERRY, *ROAR*

Sometimes a poem or a song or a book says "you" and you know who the "you" is, but sometimes not.

Sometimes you find out years later, at an afterparty for instance, and sometimes not only your memory of reading the poem or song or book is different, but your whole social life.

Sometimes someone else's book tells you the story of your own life, and you still don't know for a while that the "you" is you!

Katy Perry has more or less confessed that *Roar* is about John Mayer.

"*Roar* is a song I wrote when I was a little bit upset," Katy says, "I found myself having a break with my boyfriend who I loved very much, and it really hurt my heart."

I said to myself, 'I need to see what is going on with me and make sure I'm all good.'"

I'm really happy for her, glad she's no longer feeling hurt, glad to hear her roar.

I hope she doesn't even have to roar right now, purrs instead, pulling long on a tangerine water pipe, warm weed bubble cloaking her body like a melting marshmallow.

I know it doesn't matter who Katy's addressee "really is."

Although, for the record, she is drastically underachieving.

In *The Saga of Hallfred the Troublesome Poet,* Hallfred is a poet and berserk Viking.

When he goes to the house of his rival for a summer, he recites poetry describing him.

Hallfred doesn't name the object of these scalding lines, but everybody in the house knows who he means.

The poems brutally satirize his rival's sex life and suggest his inadequacy in the bedroom, but the metaphors are so complex, a whole hermeneutics is required to suss the dis.

"He lumbers (like a fulmar swimming) to his bed / the shearer of fjord-flame / herring-stuffed on the foam-path / before he, beguiler of scythes, unlovely, / dares to slide under the blankets."

The plucky opening synths of *Roar* only barely adumbrate its chorus, when Katy's voice becomes ferocious as a hundred big cats boasting over the torn corpse of a zebra or whatever.

Yesterday I read Dodie Bellamy's *The Feraltern,* have you read this piece?

Dodie describes tendencies in writing by working class women, like Diane Di Prima's *Loba* and Sara Larsen's *Merry Hell,* works that are uncompromising in their "wildness."

A theory of class and artmaking emerges, a theory of sublime ferocity, it's excellent to read and share this world with Dodie, Diane, and Sara.

I wondered if Katy Perry would like this theory of the feraltern as a way to describe *Roar.*

In *Roar* she describes her body as morphologically blended with wild jungle predators.

She's got "the eye of the tiger," her roar is "louder than a lion," etc.

Her triumph includes theriomorphic screams, is loud as thunder, makes the earth quake, her song is like Thor's big ass hammer.

The disastrous patriarchy permits her boyfriend to restrain and hush her, in the song and IRL, but when Katy roars, the addressee of this roar is obviously inferior; this becomes her poetics, like John Keats hated that Grecian Urn or whatever and told it so.

When the dust settles, she is a feral beast hitting the high notes, he no better than one snail turd.

In *Roar,* Katy proposes woah-oh-ohs as an onomatopoetic expression of a real roar.

Over the summer, Alli and Brandon and I went to the beach in

Alameda, it was the best.

Roar had just come out, and we listened to it in the car.

We all agreed that it was pretty good.

I liked it the best, followed by Brandon, followed by Alli, who has finally come around to Katy Perry more or less, but wasn't totally enraptured with *Roar.*

We had talked up the beach a lot over breakfast; pulling into the parking lot I hoped it was as warm and clean as it had been the last time.

That, after all, had been a swim in a pre-*Roar* world, all ecosystems on earth became unpredictable afterwards.

The water was warm and salty, tender waves of the bay buoyed our bodies in little rhythmic tufts, we washed our feet off after, three little animals covered in sand and slime.

For years I have made a joke that Brandon is my nemesis.

Our names are almost identical, and a few years ago when his book *Dark Brandon* came out, I got a lot of e-mails from people congratulating *me* on my new book, psh.

One time in Iceland this guy at a bar asked me if I was the person who wrote *Dark Brandon.*

Lucky for that guy I'm a soft breathing scallop and not Hallfred the Troublesome Poet!

Brandon, you fucking angel!

I mean, you swimming fulmar, lil herring on the foam-path!

LANA DEL REY, *SUMMERTIME SADNESS*

It's winter.

It's not "technically" winter, but here especially seasons are more feelings than weather, feelings with scant appurtenance, disrespect to all calendars.

By the time it's technically winter, the world has been wintering for a while, like going to sleep includes a time of being already asleep before you know you are.

In Oakland winter signifies its arrival with a different vocabulary.

Some say happiness is like a season, only expressible by ekphrastics and external gestures, inside there's an intransigent morphology that never quite resolves, and, anyway, like winter in Oakland, tomorrow the raindrops turn into sunburns.

Last year, on the day it technically became winter, I wrote a poem called "California" about Bernadette Mayer and winter and Joni Mitchell.

Whenever I travel, to the Midwest especially, people always ask me, "How's California?"

I always think, *California?*

Oakland only seems tangentially part of California (or even the world) although maybe California itself is like the beginning of a season, you only know what it feels like when it's right on top of you.

If I had to explain what I thought California was or how California feels I would play Joni Mitchell and Dr. Dre records for whoever asked, just like anybody would.

I love Lana Del Rey's melodrama and ennui.

When I first heard her, I thought of her as the Nancy Sinatra of present day Williamsburg, lustish, glamorous, pouty hipster sovereign of Brooklyn, walking tweet from the saddest student extra on *Gossip Girl,* suicidal emerald the loveliest and most dramatic of jewels.

The first time I heard her sing was in Ashland, Oregon.

Our friends were there, so we drove through northern California, snowy path to the ethical chapel of hanging out at Kasey's place.

We stopped in Weed, California so I could pee by a crawdad tank in the bathroom; I thought and said to the crawdads I want to write a poem as baked in California as Weed is lost.

Some say happiness is "Oh my God / I feel it in the air / telephone wires above / sizzle like a snare."

In other words, happiness is like song, it descends from somewhere above, it permeates the breath, it is literally ecstatic until you incorporate it, then it becomes immortal.

It takes a special kind of commitment to melodrama to title something *Summertime Sadness,* but to then sing a song that's not about sadness at all, except inasmuch as happiness is actually sadness, to do that is classical hubris.

"My bad baby by my *heavenly* side," Lana sings, at home in the pantheon.

She's a Gemini, the sign represented by the twins, Castor and Pollux, the drama queens of ancient Williamsburg.

When Castor died, Pollux offered to lend him his own heavenly side, now they live half the time in the land of the dead and half the time on the steppes of Olympus, I wonder if they're happy or if it's summer.

Some say there is no such thing as happiness in the halls of Hel or Valhalla or wherever.

Wordsworth writes in "The Prelude," that his concern is with "The very world which is the world of / all of us the place on which, in the end, / we find our happiness or not at all."

Happiness is tied to contingency and doomed to ephemerality, this is what makes it possible but impossible to savor, fragile as finance.

Some say that Lana Del Rey was born in a manger behind a burrito shop in Weed in order to wage war against temporariness.

In the history of ideas about happiness, people are basically divided about whether happiness is transient or lingering.

I thought about this all the time this summer, especially while smoking.

I really tried to *love* each cigarette, the few minutes they burned away, praising their essential goodness and rightness.

Momentary bursts of heaven on earth.

The abbreviated present tense of the pitifully addicted.

For addicts the future occasionally irrupts as syntax in the present as the promise of a dark time which offers little in the way of pleasure.

The future becomes the affective opposite of the famous castle in the air, the Land of No Cockaigne, Big Rock Fucked Mountain, not those beautiful places where you live on a diet of sugar and whiskey and cigarettes and never get fat or alcoholic or get lung cancer or.

Last night Alli and I watched this show about "strange addictions."

People are addicted to really strange things, it turns out.

Like eating toilet paper, and pottery, and laundry detergent, and picking up heavy objects and putting them back down again obsessively.

I'm not judging.

The disproportionate feelings I have for the protagonists of these vignettes prove my own deficit; these addictions exotic to me because I don't or can't recognize the obvious irradiating pleasure of eating a flower pot filled with cigarette butts.

I have even heard it suggested that there's nothing pleasurable about smoking cigarettes, psh.

The way I understand addiction to anything is determined by my first and most lasting addiction, listening to pop music, and I know that precisely because one song can make a total claim on one's entire desire, that virtually anything can, even Ajax umami and the dear freshness deep down laundry detergent things.

One of these people was addicted to having cats.

She had a lot of cats, worked three jobs to support these cats, she looked in the camera actually kind of jolly, she said, "Everything is cats."

MILEY CYRUS, *WE CAN'T STOP*

Yesterday was Miley Cyrus's birthday.

I saw her sing on the computer in front of a giant video cat.

When the song reached its emotional crest, the cat teared up and wept diamonds.

There's something wonderful for me about this woman who's obsessed with cats on the show about strange addictions.

I'm not obsessed with cats, but I love how casually and even cheerfully she recognizes and affirms the totalizing presence of cats in her life, how they are definitional really, with *that* I sympathize.

I suppose that another basic reason I love this cat lady in *Strange Addictions* is that while she's undeniably right, that everything really *is* cats, for her, for us, it's only almost true that everything is cats, some things are not exactly cats.

In nooks and crannies you find little smears of cat vomit, now that's cats.

Outside the house though, I dunno, non-feline forms prowl around, trying to make your party stop.

We Can't Stop is a manifesto for a party, a party so comprehensive it functions finally as a symbol for all party.

It's a travelogue too in the sense that Miley devotes much of *We Can't Stop* to describing the party's landscape.

The landscape includes red cups, sweaty bodies everywhere, hands in the air, girls with big butts [sic], people in line for the bathroom, nose cookie.

Its status as a manifesto is obvious, although the weird syntactical economy of the song subtly assimilates the phrases "we can't stop" and "we won't stop" as if they were similes.

"We won't stop" is the expected declaration of the party, uttered in defiance of whatever straw or flesh cop might come with an injunction to pause.

"We can't stop," on the other hand, is pathetic.

To the same degree that "we won't stop" insists on autonomy, "we can't stop" admits bondage.

The dominant expression of this curiously uncontrollable autonomy is that the party determines and reinforces the social roles of the house.

"We run things / things don't run we" is the way in which Miley associates what is home-ly with the economic.

Her refusal to conform to the grammatically correct "us" is a further expression of her iconoclasm, but her refusal to assimilate the pronoun into the accusative also reinforces her absolute dominance over the house.

There *is* something fucked up about my, and Miley's, occasional expression of desire for unchecked pleasure.

We both thirst, our anthropophagous impulses appear innocent but are symptomatic of a terrible metabolism.

Frenching a vinegar sponge, licking ooze off lips, jutting tongue for more.

We have decided to not to die; we want to continue, Miley and I; we wash and pray in our way and quit smoking and wag our butts out because we know how easy it is for a body to stop; we can and we will stop and until then we want to resist that immanent enervation; we both abuse melody to do it.

I took a long bath while she partied somewhere.

So selfish, I barely gave her continued existence a single thought.

After my bath I did a search for "Miley Cyrus birthday" as a sort of penance; I don't recommend it.

Let me just take that one for you.

One thing you'll see if you do make this treacherous effort is a page emblazoned "Miley Scarfs Down Big Penis Cake."

Really, resist the temptation to see this for yourself.

I didn't even take the opportunity to wonder how her party went; it must have been wonderful, I wonder if it has stopped or was able to stop.

I lifted my back from the bottom of the tub so that the water which rushed into the space my back had occupied was newly hot.

A few days ago there was a night of "insane" wind; it ripped trees out of the ground and made my building shudder.

Some small leaves blew into the bathroom through an open window, and when the bath was full of water I saw some remnants of the storm floating in the water.

I had a real Wordsworth moment in there, looking around the bath and my body and the little pieces of leaves, suddenly even my beloved bathtub became a hall of pain, me all wet in there, crying out *was it all for this?*

Not that I've ever had to do anything really.

Not that Miley Cyrus has ever had to do anything.

I pinched both nipples as hard as I could, winced, stood up, dried off, streaked toner across my face, said the quickest prayer for eternal youth or youth-ish, then listened to *We Can't Stop* a dozen times, bending my knees into it, supplicating with every effort of reverence.

Each time I listened to it it appeared more and more mythological.

More and more an analogical instance of grace.

I can't and won't stop looking into the face of that sad cat, it *was* all for this.

ANNA KENDRICK, *CUPS*

Bernadette Mayer wrote, "What was strange was the need to review, re-read, re-use, recycle what had already been written.

My own work was never finished and it was always leading back to itself and older work.

Not a system of feedback but a system of feeding."

Maybe this is what Anna Kendrick has done too, nourished by the Carter Family's *When I'm Gone,* singing *Cups.*

Cups is also known as *Cups (When I'm Gone).*

When I'm Gone was first recorded by the Carter Family in 1931 and is attributed to Carter Family patriarch A.P. Carter, but you never know.

In 1928, when Carter fully realized the fiscal potential of writing, recording, and most importantly copyrighting tunes, he began the process of "collecting" songs in southwest Virginia.

That same year, he met Leslie Riddle, an African-American man who "helped" him "collect" these songs.

Riddle would memorize the melody and lyrics of the songs, prompting Carter to call him "a human tape recorder."

In other cases, the Carter Family played, recorded and of course profited off of original compositions that Riddle wrote himself.

Soon after, Riddle disappears from the historical record, completing this miniature of United States history.

Compared to the ad hoc corporations many of the songs on America's Top 40 are, *Cups* has the innocent atmosphere of a stubborn mom'n'pop in some burgeoning Midwestern suburban sprawl, surviving hypermarts which surround it, hungry to feed on its corpse.

It's set on a threshold, a lover is about to leave.

So much of pop music is set on this very threshold.

Every time a lover leaves in a song it's an allegory for a final abandonment, by extension a metaphor for the death of the lover.

Hence, "You're gonna miss me when I'm gone" expresses the certainty on the lover's part that the beloved will possess an imminent lack, like the bitter possession of debt, the future separation, permanent break, the irrevocable absence of death.

I'm reading this book *Agonistic Poetry* by William Fitzgerald.

When I got it from the library, I remembered that I had checked it out before, and had talked with Stacy about it, as the book is about Pindar, and Stacy and I frequently read about Pindar and talked about his poetry.

In the front flap of the book, there's a taped sheet of paper that shows the history of the book's circulation.

It's been checked out exactly three times—by me, in 2005, by Stacy a few months later, and now me again, in 2013.

I wiped the little sheet across the skin of my face, in case there were any still aspirating molecules of sloughed tissue.

The cups in *Cups* are cups of whiskey I guess, morose accompaniments to loneliness, lingering souvenirs of desertion.

From now on, I plan to steal, I mean "collect," something from everybody I love while they're alive.

I will start with the bathrooms of poets.

Don't worry about inviting me over, it'll be something small I promise, like a Band-Aid or a Vicodin.

Actually, not a Vicodin, because the point would be to try to collect something and save it.

Vicodin have very abbreviated lifespans in my house, the central reason I never seek them out.

On a little sill above my records I have a few strewn charms; a teabag from Stacy's office, a wet wipe from Huitrerie Regis, Go Go's 45 vacation all I ever wanted, the postcard Evan sent from Italy of Caravaggio's *Incredulity of St. Thomas* on which he's written you *are* America's next top model!

I wanted *Agonistic Poetry* to be about the history of how poets in English read and attempted to emulate Pindar.

The meters of Pindar are of course totally unsympathetic to replication in English verse.

My interest in these poets is an extension of a basic greenwash, a repetition of the impulse to gum a can and say how it tastes.

Pindar is really interested in the relationship of poetry and glory, which is a way of saying collective memory.

Part of his commercial packaging for the poem is to present it as a multidimensional remembrance machine that exists shining into perpetuity.

Which is I guess what *Cups* is up to as well.

The impassioned belief that song can try and substitute for bodies when they leave.

Whether they leave in desperate *ecstasis* to mark the end of a bad association, whether they go to Hel or Valhalla, we miss them when they're gone.

I'm going to miss you when you're gone.

The poem is decidedly better than a Vicodin.

After all, a Vicodin dissipates into the pleasure receptors of the tongue, making everything okay for a number of hours, but leaves no souvenirs when it's gone.

MACKLEMORE AND RYAN LEWIS ft. MARY LAMBERT, *SAME LOVE*

Although *Same Love* seems to thematize homogeneity, its verses and chorus have totally incommensurate registers.

In the verses, Macklemore delivers a set of discursive juridico-theological principles about queer relationships.

His theory is at once liberal, scientific, and Christian.

It states that queer love is essentially "the same" as the straight love he is doomed to experience as the sole source of transcendent pleasure in his life.

Before you start feeling sorry for him, he quickly reaffirms the "natural" imminence of his own straight sexual drive by reminding us how great he was at t-ball or whatever.

Mary Lambert's chorus on the other hand is a sweet and pretty paean to the love of her life.

Her love is imminent too, but her plaint is a poem to Macklemore's hack prose.

In Plato's *Lysis,* one of the ideas that Socrates and the two hotties consider is whether the friend attraction is based on "like to like."

Socrates and his sexist friends don't think relationships with women count as relationships.

So you can imagine him asking Macklemore a bunch of annoying questions about his little Same Love theory.

It's hard to imagine anybody writing down the transcript of that conversation.

Fuck I miss smoking.

Most of my friends who heard *Same Love* were sort of "Thanks but no thanks, Macklemore," I get it.

After listening to *Same Love* dozens of times, he still just sounds like a smug liberal prick, sooo satisfied with his own expansive tolerance.

But I do wonder if my powerful instinct to reject Macklemore and all things Macklemorean is due to a suspicion that we are perhaps alike, he and I.

I am not a Macklemore to myself, but perhaps to others my actually existing solidarity appears hollow.

Fuck, you guys I am really feeling it!

We also have similar haircuts.

I guess finally I don't know for sure what solidarity is.

Can it take the form of yearning, can it be a kind of melody, does it only refer to the immediate self-sacrifice of the body in the moment perceived to be the critical one?

If so, okay, but what if we disagree that the critical moment has arrived, or disappeared, how can we be sure?

Maybe solidarity is like friendship, always in dispute until the moment in which it either has to be true or false.

Mary Lambert's part is so pretty.

When her voice thins and moans, "No crying on Sundays," pearls cluster at the sides of my pupils, my wrinkles dew.

As a kid, America's Top 40 was the only good thing about Sundays, the rest was misery.

Not misery I guess, although Sunday afternoon was frequently the theater for confrontation between my father and I.

He was probably aggravated by being dragged to the church as much or more than I was.

I was just bored, the ruthless and jealous God I feared and loved rarely made an appearance amidst the Lutherans.

He used the hour to balance his checkbook and stare off into space.

Once, fighting with my dad after a service, I vowed to end my life, emptied a bottle of Tylenol out on the kitchen counter and started shoveling them into my mouth.

The problem, besides the fact that it would have taken a *lot* of Tylenol to bring about the liver failure necessary to kill me, was that I was no good at taking pills.

I gagged and expectorated, chucked up little rubies all over; my dad stood around looking amused.

There was a lot of crying on those Sundays.

The last hour of America's Top 40 brought about contradictory feelings.

On one hand, these songs are the best of the best.

On the other, I would always feel stupidly impatient to know what song would be the *best*.

In *Same Love*, Mary Lambert names two attributes of love.

Love is patient, love is kind.

Now I see David almost every Sunday and never listen to *America's Top 40*.

He is always coming from church, and I try to remember to ask him if there was anything special that he heard or learned that day.

I asked him yesterday, and he told me that the sermon had been about patience.

CAPITAL CITIES, *SAFE AND SOUND*

At the café, I was telling David about my book *Top Forty,* and he said, how long has it been since you read Rousseau's *Confessions?*

He was sweet to think I'd ever read it or anything else, thanks David.

I just got it from the library, it's so good.

In the first chapter Rousseau remembers a song sung by his aunt when he was a child.

It reads, "I strive in vain to account for the strange effect which that song has on my heart, but I cannot explain why I am moved.

All I know is that I am quite incapable of singing it to the end without breaking into ears."

Obviously it should read "breaking into tears."

Somebody underlined "ears" and wrote next to it in pencil, "ha!"

And it *is* funny, but "breaking into ears" is actually pretty good too, if not better, do you agree?

I doubt that *Safe and Sound* will ever provide such tears for anybody, provoked by the memory of its melody, gait, message, but we all know that madeleinization has no relation to quality or predictability, so it's possible.

Anyway, it's not like *Safe and Sound* is a total disaster, although disaster is its primary concern.

It's winter and now it's completely dark when my alarm rings.

Alli hates it.

When the alarm rings and she's sleeping over, I grope towards her in the darkness and say, "What time do you need to get up baby?"

This question is often answered by a sweet soliloquy, fairly sophisticated for somebody fast asleep, attempting to persuade me that I shouldn't get up and walk to work, that it's, in fact, "unnatural" to consider such a course of action.

I'm usually okay when I wake up; I like the opposite-day stoniness of it, bumbling along stupefied, oafing to the bathroom, prying up the light, dreamily peeing.

This morning I woke up from a terrible dream, in which I loudly and publicly talked shit about a dear friend to the person I'm "in hate" with, ugh.

In the dream, I referred to my real life friend as "boss of the sewer flower."

In the bath I repeated the phrase over and over again so I could remember it and write it down.

It's kind of a kenning, "sewer flower" suggesting the world itself, blossoming muck reiterated through the bodies of its animals.

Safe and Sound is an invitation to love, its pitch essentially that entering into a love relationship with the singer will provide safety against an array of disasters.

These potential disasters are ecologico-magical.

They include the sky falling down, rivers drying up, hurricanes of frowns, death, a "tidal wave of mystery" which I always heard as a "tidal wave of misery," sewer suffocating its little buds.

Like "bursting into ears," "tidal wave of misery" seems better than "tidal wave of mystery."

The singer suggests that if you only return his love you'll both be safe and sound.

I thought about saying that while these disasters are all ecological, none of them are "natural" because there are no "natural" disasters, but James reminds me that even Satan and capitalism are human inventions and thus, in that sense, "natural."

Still, it's a comforting thought that our lovers will keep us safe and sound.

Alli and I talk all the time about what if there's an earthquake and we're apart, what our plan is.

What's your plan?

Sometimes I daydream about the walk, from my shattered room to our rendezvous, it's full of fires, people screaming, sputtering sewer lines overflowing into flowerbeds, but there is also the most effervescent camaraderie.

The latent meaning of *Safe and Sound* is that pop itself will keep us safe and sound, but I dunno.

Maybe from the "hurricane of frowns" and "tidal wave of mystery," but what about the big earthquake or the hurricane of wind and water or white supremacy?

Probably not I guess.

We are living together in a sewer flower, my friends, we are eating turd honey.

Some say pop precisely fails to reflect the miserable conditions of the real world, is instead a regime of highly addictive distractions, candied loops that desensitize its adherents to the stifling devastation of the world pop traffics in and which it helps to make.

But if *Safe and Sound* won't keep us safe and sound, and if the poem and the painting and the syntagm "I love you" won't keep us safe and sound, and if we want to be safe and sound, what are we left with, the cops?

I guess we relinquish safety and soundness altogether, band together in the "adaptable, fluctuating, unstable" world Francesca talked about in her talk on revolutionary tenderness.

"I have come to believe that revolutionary tenderness signifies 'the negation of the negation,'" she writes.

"That is, the refusal of the shittiness of our present moment, the determined insistence on optimism."

Ryan Merchant and Sebu Simonian, the guys in Capital Cities, met each other on craigslist, a notoriously unsafe and unsound way to meet a stranger, but I guess so far their optimism is working out okay for them.

CALVIN HARRIS ft. ELLIE GOULDING, *I NEED YOUR LOVE*

No offense to Ellie Goulding, but whenever I hear her sing I imagine a little imp, wee *dvargr* dwelling in lush verdure, deep inside a misty cave, enchanting travelers with her cute and throaty song.

Her voice is so wan and vulnerable, it sounds like anything could swarm and trample over it, shatter it into a mess of peeps and squeaks.

I'm in love with how it sounds and her of course.

Ellie Goulding is from Lyonshall, a small rural town in England near the Welsh border.

She's the most famous person to come from Lyonshall ever.

Calvin Harris is from Dumfries, in Scotland, and the most famous person to come from Dumfries is either Calvin Harris or the poet Robert Burns, depending on who you ask I guess.

I'm from Kearney, a small rural town in Missouri, and except for the outlaw Jesse James, I am probably the most famous person to ever come from Kearney, which is obviously not saying much.

It makes me feel close to Ellie Goulding, like we could really bond about our humble beginnings and supernova maturity.

I'm sure if we did meet I would just stutter, and she would feel sorry for me in her urbane and sophisticated way.

"Sophisticated" derives from the Greek word *sophos,* meaning "wise," but *sophos* too was a way of simply saying "melody" in Ancient Greece.

Some think pop music is a desiccated shucked husk, a thanatic façade for the violence of finance, but I remember that our philosophical tradition began with the thought that melody is wise.

I Need Your Love is an extended expression of one fundamental need.

That's already smart, as knowing what you need is intelligent.

Some might argue that love isn't a suitable object of "need" or might try to argue with Ellie Goulding that she *needs* food and water and shelter, but she merely *wants* love.

But I dunno.

Anybody who has ever felt a Ragnarok of the upper breast over somebody understands that reciprocated love can be as essential to self-reproduction as any calories.

Just ask Hallfred the Troublesome Poet, he needed love so bad that even when his lips were lopped off in a gruesome meadow he was like "I love you."

I need a haircut, I need to pee, I need a glass of Chardonnay, I need to assuage this soft extraretinal apocalypse, I need your love.

It makes me laugh to say that I'm the other famous person from Kearney, Missouri.

I can already guess that when Alli reads it she will say omigod, you can't say that in your poem, it's so arrogant.

The person I thought was really famous was the guy who cut my hair at the town's one barber shop.

He happened to have the same name as a real famous person, Kevin Cline.

Kevin cut hair for a living, but he was a country musician with aspirations for astral metamorphosis, I mean he dreamt himself in that Ole Opry, god's grandeur twanging through him.

He had recorded an album which had been pressed onto vinyl, that was more than enough to win my awe.

I can't remember what the album was called, but the cover showed him sitting in his barber chair, kicked back, one denim ankle draped over the other, a dusty and powerful mullet, sunglasses, something drooping out of his mouth.

A strand of hay or a cigarette I guess.

He would play the album on repeat while cutting white brats' hair all day, fuck the other barber must have hated it.

At the town's annual festival, Jesse James Days, Kevin performed as a one-man band.

I spent most of my day today looking for any shred of evidence of his career in reliquary form on the Internet, it does not appear to exist.

Did I make him up?

The determination with which the singer in *I Need Your Love* needs the love approaches the object of the love as if it's an addictive substance.

I need a cigarette, I need a Vicodin, I need to hear *I Need Your Love*, I need the umami of common household cleaners to coat my tongue and throat, I need a ride, I need your love.

The tongue is the house of taste I guess.

Bernadette Mayer writes, "There are some motherfuckers I would like to show a star to."

As the soft civil war we read as history brings down a torch to Lyonshall and Dumfries and Kearney, who will be the singer of our deeds, Ellie?

I may be disappointing everyone with my temporary descent into boastfulness, but it's not like I'm acting like Jesse James.

That murderous slavery-loving prick Jesse James.

When I was a teenager some scientists came to town and dug up his body, so they could perform mitochondrial analysis of his DNA.

My neighbors across the street made t-shirts to sell to the small flocks of tourists who wanted—maybe even *needed*—to see that old shabby coffin get pulled up out of the dirt.

The t-shirts read "I Dig Jesse," sigh.

I anticipate the complete and utter destruction of these t-shirts, of

Jesse James's mitochondrial DNA, of the ephemeral transitory museum known as America's Top 40, but I want *I Need Your Love* to survive, I need *I Need Your Love* to survive.

IMAGINE DRAGONS, *RADIOACTIVE*

A few days ago Larry wrote, "Y'all be acting like this cold weather ain't a chance to look cute…" as a caption to a stellar selfie.

This made me laugh; Larry looked great in his winter coat, I also thought I looked pretty cute in my coat this morning.

When I leave for work, I usually walk a block before I put my headphones on.

I spare the time to anticipate the day ahead.

The reason it only takes a minute to complete this exercise is that once I get off the train and go into my office I sit there for nine hours, with some variety of stimuli and task, some room for miracle or happenstance; but finally perform a toxic repetition of gestures and behaviors under the duress of missing human contact.

When I turn the corner onto 14th Street there's a long and high windowpane that stretches across a big building, half a block or so.

I pause and consider my reflection, make sure nothing is weird.

Radioactive is also set in the morning, and also includes sartorial considerations.

The details of its temporal setting are convincing, but its eschatology is marked by a pervasive mischrony.

That is, the features of its specific apocalyptic vision are steadfastly twentieth century.

That's the way it sounds, too, classic rock melodrama of self-abolition, stone gate built against the pleasure of smelly morning dewdrops.

They're so desperately serious about their psychic turmoil that it just makes me want to tickle these guys.

That's right, Dan #1, Ben, Dan #2, Wayne, I'm gonna tickle you!!!!

So many pop songs are set on temporal thresholds and liminal spaces, sleeping, waking up, leaving, coming in, falling off or rising up.

I guess they're there to teach us how to recognize and negotiate these thresholds in our own lives; they tell us to open our mouths and sing when we find ourselves there.

Dan #1 says, "*Radioactive,* to me, is a very masculine, powerful-sounding song.

There's a lot of personal story behind it, but generally speaking, it's a song about having an awakening.

Kind of waking up one day and deciding to do something new, and see life in a fresh way."

Okay, but given that *Radioactive* describes familiar apocalyptic circumstances, what is "fresh" about the features of this posthuman landscape?

The singer wakes up "to ash and dust," breathes in chemicals, suggesting massive ecological catastrophe.

We next meet him on a prison bus, "raising flags" and getting dressed in supposedly "revolutionary" colors, not insignificantly red.

By the third verse, the vision has moved on from the destructive armature of worldwide crisis to the regenerative community founded in its wake.

The way Imagine Dragons express this is, "The sun hasn't died / deep in my bones / straight from inside."

Or should I say "the Imagine Dragons," as if Dan #1, Ben, Dan #2, and Wayne are themselves individual dragons?

I wonder if they know how cute they sound when they sing with such solemnity and torpor, "Welcome to the new age," like do you imagine them with their fierce haircuts and jowly grimaces secretly rubbing crystals and swabbing tinctures, rubbing each other's chests with mustard oil?

I would like to send them all copies of Kathy Acker's *Empire of the Senseless* for another take on apocalypse and new age.

And then tickle them all senseless!!!

This song was so big for so many people this year, it suggests that this 21st century apocalypse is totally relevant, thriving, meaningful.

Except for one little cold week, winter has been mild and dry.

I heard someone say, "This is a *very* enjoyable apocalypse."

I guess all of the people who thought the world would end in fire are basically right.

In *Radioactive*, there are just a bunch of human beings and vehicles, sole traffic of the end times.

When Snorri Sturluson writes about what the apocalypse looks like in *Prose Edda*, there are all kinds of animals.

A grim and bloody rooster crows.

The wolf Garmr, shackled in front of a cave for centuries, snaps his handcuffs.

Sturluson writes, "Brothers will fight / and kill each other, / sister's children / will defile kinship.

It is harsh in the world, / whoredom rife, / it is an axe age, a sword age, / shields are riven, / it is a wind age, a wolf age / before the world goes headlong.

No man will have mercy on another."

Part of me hopes this present phase of the world's collapse extends as long as possible, until all the Imagine Dragons and I are long dissipated into tiny radioactive molecules, looking like us but invisible, in brilliant coats, playing winter baseball in the park, the Coho survive somehow, etc.; I hope Snorri Sturluson and the Imagine Dragons are wrong about the axes and the prison buses, I hope the news is wrong about the Coho.

My coat is too cute to burn and turn into ash.

MAROON FIVE, *LOVE SOMEBODY*

If anything good will come of writing my book *Top Forty* it might be that listening to *Love Somebody* so many times will finally cure me of a longstanding allergy to Adam Levine's singing voice.

If Nate Ruess sounds like, what was it again, "a bloodless chestnut"?

Then Levine's voice is a cyborg Labrador, fabricated in the laboratory of unrepentant capital to diminish the history of human pleasure.

Nothing matters less than my disdain for Levine's voice; I should and do grovel at his Gucci loafers.

I admit however that it is hard to imagine a future in which this song comes on and I do anything but shudder and skip.

But I dunno, you can't tell the future finally.

The ear is like the tongue, and taste like all tautologies only appears in the present tense.

There is no gustatory oracular, and taste has no real history.

Because we cannot tell the future, it's all the more difficult to tell the present, despite the efforts of America's Top 40, the stock exchange, all avant gardes.

It is impossible to know the meaning of a single twerk.

It's even hard to tell what season it is in Oakland.

Fernand Braudel wrote, "Financialization is a sign of Autumn."

Epigonal feelings, undeniably sexy as they are, are too confident; who can say how late we are, we might be later than that; we might be babes?

I know it's winter because I'm cold, because the light grows sparer and sparer on both sides of the working day, because I'm wearing this beautiful coat.

Love Somebody was #3 on America's Top 40 the week of September 14.

Now it's months later and it's gone from the chart, as are most of the songs I've written about in this book; only the most stubborn remain.

The fundamental mystery of *Love Somebody* is about what or who exactly it is the singer claims to want to love.

On one hand, he just wants to love somebody.

On the other hand, there's a shadowy "you" who occasionally supplants the indefinite 3rd person pronoun, a you contrary to the anonymity of "somebody," the singer's great intimate rather.

It doesn't help clarify anything that the song takes place on the dance floor at night, a time and place famous for fleeting feelings to appear as epic love stories.

The slippage from "I just wanna love *somebody*" to "I'll think about *you* every single day" expresses a key truth about pop music.

Because pop songs are for us, because they're for reiteration in our mouths and in our keys, because they're made for us to gather together and sing with each other, because they're meant to condition and inflect how we reflect on our own indeterminate and affective experiences, it hardly matters who the "you" is in something like *Love Somebody*.

The substitutability of the definite 2nd person pronoun and the indefinite 3rd person pronoun depends on the site of our performance, who we dream of is somebody, anybody, whoever, or whether we speak to you.

You are the last word in the syntagm "I love you."

You are what binds us in the sentence, the one we're dancing around and singing with.

But the future of the sentence can never be known.

It's that uncertainty that Levine refers to when he sings the bridge, "I don't know what to do, I'm right in front of you / Asking you to stay, you should stay, stay with me tonight, yeah."

This wish swiftly moves from a question ("asking you to stay") to a hortatory ("you should stay") to the imperative ("stay with me tonight") in one sequence.

The imperative is the mood of present tense certainty about the future, it pretends to leave no room for accident or disobedience.

Likewise, the speaker of the imperative is always alone, whereas the hortatory is grammatically plural, "Let's go."

But it does not predict the future, we can always say no, even with a foot on our esophagi.

Is it the suredness of songs like *Love Somebody* which trick us into thinking we can divine future events?

So we talk about "stringing people (capitalists) up," about slitting throats in Oscar Grant Plaza, joke about the server who was smashed in the face with a brick during a demonstration.

This may seem like I think the imperative is the Adam Levine of moods.

But I dunno.

If there are lips near my ear I want a tongue to insist.

I want little hairs of my real and fleshy ears licked, remanded, bestirred.

I want clear dimensional *I want you to love me* panted all over my neck and collar.

Not anybody's voice, not Caesar's or Obama's or Adam Levine's.

Your lips.

You know who you are.

ZEDD ft. FOXES, *CLARITY*

Clarity is structured around two sets of oppositions, "tragedy" vs. "remedy" and "insanity" vs. "clarity."

Both are a little unusual as oppositions, like you might think the opposites of these would be more like…comedy, poison, sanity, confusion?

But no.

For Foxes and Zedd, their complex sensibilities insist that their love is healing disaster, illuminating and mad, all at the same time.

Sara said something so smart at Joel's talk on *The Communist Manifesto*.

About how we cathect to capitalism like an abused lover.

That we tragically, insanely interiorize a feeling of immanence about this relationship, despite capital's notorious fantasies of collapse and apocalypse, we believe in an "us" til the end, against our better interests.

In other words, we interiorize a feeling that there is no world without our being together.

I think about that all the time, thanks Sara.

Joshua Clover wrote, "Pop songs are smarter than us; they know what they can and cannot do.

We have less choice; we must destroy this world or die."

Sometimes I daydream about the world dying, shoring up my knees in bathwater, looking up at the clock face count down bathtime.

In this dream I illogically survey the dead world, survivor somehow.

Some say that when we destroy the world we will have to destroy Zedd and Foxes and *Clarity*, the particular narcosis they've made their lives' work is precisely antithetical to our efforts to destroy the world so it can be new.

But I dunno.

I actually have started to think that Zedd and Foxes and *Clarity* might be in love with me, that I'm their remedy and clarity as much as they are mine, and each other's.

AAnd when that creepy Ragnarok rooster makes the trees blaze with his beak, we'll find each other for succor, get in the bath, all three of us, Zedd, Foxes, me, four if you include the rooster, it'll be like in *Melancholia*, that fun.

Okay, maybe they're not "in love with me."

Maybe, at least, they have my better interests in mind.

Can that be a premise of our communism, to try and have everybody's better interest in mind?

For some, our communism includes "stringing people (capitalists) up," slitting throats in Oscar Grant Plaza, smashing servers with bricks and laughing about the brick-smashed servers.

For me it includes *Clarity*.

Clarity opens with a few repeating notes, simple synths that hardly foreshadow how explosive the track will become.

These songs always make Alli laugh; when I play them for her she says, "I wonder what the chorus is gonna sound like?"

It's true, their predictability makes their choruses a bit anticlimactic, as they detonate into Mykonos beach parties of tragedy, remedy, insanity, clarity.

"Clarity" derives from Latin *clarus* which is a weirder and more ambiguous word than "clarity" is in English, in that it means both "shining" and "clear."

Because shine is opaque, shine is a bulwark against visibility.

Maybe clarity is like pop itself, something so sheer it takes effort to discern, like you know how crystals are full of secrets.

George Oppen knew about this riddle of *clarus,* he wrote, "Clarity in the sense of *silence.*"

George Oppen loved silence, loved clarity, was rich enough to buy a long and quiet time full of clear and silent thought.

I'm not trying to hate on George Oppen.

I just mean that I dive into frozen waves and the past comes back to life.

And I'm mowing a lawn, butt in water every morning, buckled in a still whip listening to hearing Casey Kasem say numbers, widening, clarifying, whitening, wrinkling, the whole time I have headphones on; the voices inside them keep saying they have my better interests in mind.

I'm a disaster literally, there are broken stars in me, Zedd and Foxes are in there with a bunch of glue.

Our manifesto is called *There Are Some Motherfuckers I Would Like To Show A Star To.*

The manifesto is a tragedy, it is probiotic, it gets crazy, goes nuts, is subtitled *Your Better Interests.*

Listen to Kathy Acker.

Listen to Zedd, Foxes, *Clarity,* clarity, listen hard for the lullabies composed of our Communism.

Sorry, I mean, "Let's listen to them together."

ROBIN THICKE ft. PHARRELL and T.I., *BLURRED LINES*

In *Bring It On* (2000, dir. Peyton Reed), Torrance Shipman is the new captain of the 5-time national champion cheerleading squad from Rancho Cucamonga High.

She has been named captain by the outgoing captain, known only as "Big Red," an allusion to the color and size of her hair.

Like so many films made in 1999 and 2000 the soundtrack is unapologetically and unironically populated by admirers and imitators of Blink 182.

Near the beginning of the film, Torrance meets Cliff, a cute pop punk boy in black Chucks, and his sister Missy, a talented gymnast with a bad attitude.

Torrance's political and cultural naiveté is proved when she asks Cliff, in reference to his shirt, "The Clash…is that your band or something?"

Rancho Cucamonga High is depicted as overwhelmingly white and upper class.

Indeed there's a leitmotif which might be read as suggesting that Torrance and the other students at RCH are, uh, like Nazis?

I dunno.

At one point Courtney, a soft foil on the squad, has an argument in which she suggests that Torrance is acting like a "cheertator" and that her reign is not a "cheermocracy."

In the same scene, Courtney and her friend Whitney speculate that Missy is an "Uber-dyke" and may be "from Romania."

By now every time I see the RCH on their uniforms I think of the word "Reich."

Missy agrees to join the cheerleading squad, but at their first practice she abruptly packs her bags and begins to walk out of the gym.

When Torrance confronts her by her car, Missy says, "I'm not about stealing. You ripped off those cheers!"

Torrance denies it.

Moments later the two of them are in the LA freeway system.

They arrive at East Compton High, where their cheerleading squad, the Clovers, is performing the very routine which Torrance and her cohort had been practicing.

Torrance is crushed.

As they leave the gym, the captain of the Clovers, Isis, leads her squad out to the parking lot, following Torrance and Missy.

"Ya'll enjoy the show?" she asks them, "Were the ethnic festivities to your liking today?"

Isis explains that she has seen Rancho Cucamonga cheerleaders in her gym before, "Ya'll come up here, steal our routines, put blonde hair on it, and win trophies."

Torrance again denies knowledge of any theft, but frantically tries for days to confirm whether this had really been the case.

She laments, "My entire cheerleading career has been a lie."

Missy tries to comfort her, "Well, at least it's just cheerleading."

But Torrance is inconsolable, "I *am* cheerleading."

When she finally reaches her philandering boyfriend Aaron at college, he attempts to ease Torrance's anxiety, "It's no big deal, everybody uses each other's material—it's like this unwritten rule or something."

What Aaron is referring to as an "unwritten rule" is the long history of artists repeating, recycling, reusing other artworks in order to become less confused about their own art.

And yet, in the context of *Bring It On,* he seems to specifically reference the long history in the US of white appropriation of black art, which regularly elides the visibility of that appropriation.

Aaron's advice in the end is to hire Sparky Polastri, a pasty choreographer of some repute, to assist the squad with developing an original white routine.

Polastri arrives, abuses the cheerleaders, and after some violence and intimidation, instructs them in an ostensibly unique, white routine.

However, in a dismaying turn of events for the squad, Polastri has taught this very same routine to a competing school!

The other squad performs it first at regionals, leaving the Rancho Cucamonga squad no choice but to out themselves as uncreative consumers.

The girls and guys on East Compton's squad watch from the wings and laugh, temporarily satisfied with this modicum of revenge.

When it looks like the Clovers won't have the money to go to the Nationals, Torrance convinces her dad to fundraise at his office for their travel.

This "philanthropic" move shows character development for Torrance, who earlier in the film leads a cheer against a less wealthy school's squad which goes, "That's all right / that's okay / you're gonna pump our gas someday."

When she shows up at East Compton with a check, Isis is like no thanks, rips it up.

Meanwhile, Torrance and her friends develop their own routine, drawing on a variety of genres to make something saltine white.

At nationals, they perform this routine, it goes pretty well.

Not well enough to beat East Compton, who win first prize.

When Cliff asks Torrance how second place feels, she reflects for a moment before answering.

Then she says, "It feels like first."

ROOF BOOKS
the best in language since 1976

Recent & Selected Titles

• THE MEDEAD by Fiona Templeton. 314 p. $19.95
• LYRIC SEXOLOGY VOL. 1 by Trish Salah. 138 p. $15.95
• INSTANT CLASSIC by erica kaufman 90 p. $14.95
• A MAMMAL OF STYLE by Kit Robinson
& Ted Greenwald. 96 p. $14.95
• VILE LILT by Nada Gordon. 114 p. $14.95
• DEAR ALL by Michael Gottlieb. 94 p. $14.95
• FLOWERING MALL by Brandon Brown. 112 p. $14.95.
• MOTES by Craig Dworkin. 88 p. $14.95
• APOCALYPSO by Evelyn Reilly. 112 p. $14.95
• BOTH POEMS by Anne Tardos. 112 p. $14.95
• AGAINST PROFESSIONAL SECRETS by César Vallejo.
Translated by Joseph Mulligan.
(complete Spanish/English) 104 p. $14.95.

Roof Books are published by
Segue Foundation
300 Bowery • New York, NY 10012
For a complete list,
please visit our website at roofbooks.com

Roof Books are distributed by
SMALL PRESS DISTRIBUTION
1341 Seventh Street • Berkeley, CA. 94710-1403.
Phone orders: 800-869-7553
spdbooks.org